T0046162

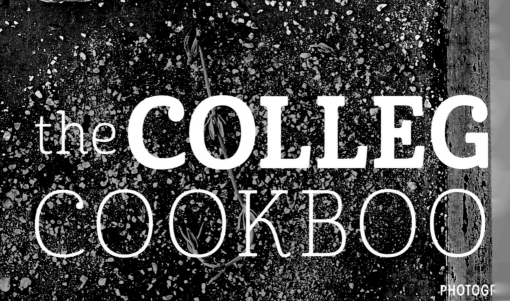

the COLLEGE

COOKBOO

PHOTOGR
AUBRI

weldon**ov**

CONTENTS

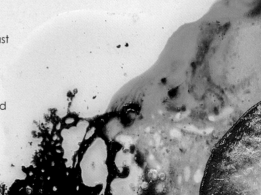

COOKING 101

Now that you've worked so hard to get into college, there's no reason why a lack of time, money, or culinary know-how should prevent you from eating well. Consider the old adage, "Necessity is the mother of invention." Mix it with "Variety is the spice of life" and the typical college cook comes into view. You're a creative and resourceful bunch with lots of ideas, an increasingly sophisticated palate, and the enterprising impatience of youth. Even if you have never so much as lifted a wooden spoon, this clever collection of hacks, tips, shortcuts, and easy-to-master recipes will have you cooking up tasty meals in minutes. Whether your objective is to eat like royalty on a pauper's budget or to ready a meal in less time than it takes to walk to the dining hall, and whether your cooking space is limited to a microwave and a mini-fridge or you have access to a full kitchen, there are quick and delicious recipes for every culinary ambition and cookery configuration.

The first lesson to learn is how to cook smart, mastering deficiencies in time, budget, and cooking knowledge by choosing recipes that suit your schedule, your wallet, and your personal taste. For meals that can be made in seconds, note prep and cooking time, look for the recipes with limited ingredients, and try the full range of microwavable options in these pages, as well as our ideas for transforming store-bought ingredients into Instagram-worthy dishes. There are dozens of cost-efficient make-ahead options, including tips for batch-cooking, easy storage, recipe shortcuts, and how to stretch a single ingredient (think roast chicken, marinated tri-tip, and pulled pork) to cover several meals. Our food shopping and pantry strategies will also help keep your spending in check. Once you've decided what to cook, our simple instructions, easy hacks, and ready variations will have you turning out delicious dishes.

Let the following pages be your guide to creating mouthwatering dishes sure to satisfy any palate—even ones with vegan, vegetarian, or gluten-free diets in mind. Experienced cooks and novice chefs alike will benefit from the step-by-step techniques, inspired variations, time-saving tips, and no-fail recipes in this comprehensive collection. With 5 minutes to cook or 50, holding $2 in your wallet or $20, the more than 100 recipes in this collection will amply satisfy the demands of the college cook while offering the types of dishes you can carry forward for a lifetime of cooking discovery.

KITCHEN BASICS

The college kitchen needs little more than a few essential tools, and the college pantry really only the bare necessities. However, there's no time like the present to begin collecting the best tools and ingredients for cooking now and in the years to come.

Building Your Tool Chest

The most essential implement in any cook's arsenal is an 8- or 10-inch chef's knife. Choose one from a quality manufacturer that feels good in your hand. It will likely be the tool you use more than any other. A small paring knife and a serrated bread knife will also be helpful, as well as a good cutting board upon which to use them. For cooking, a small and a large frying pan, a metal spatula and tongs, a small saucepan, and a large pot for pasta and soups should be adequate for most of your cooking needs. A rimmed baking sheet is useful for baking, as are baking dishes in a few sizes. For mixing, you'll need a few bowls of varying sizes, one or two wooden spoons, a whisk, a silicone spatula, and a set of measuring cups and spoons. More necessary basics include a grater-shredder and a sieve. For microwave cooking, make sure to have a few microwave-safe bowls, plates, and a mug on hand.

For some of the recipes in this book, you will also need a few small appliances. A blender is a necessity for soups and smoothies. and an electric mixer can be helpful if you like to bake.

Stocking Your Pantry

Decide what to purchase for your kitchen pantry by first considering what you like to cook. Start by selecting ingredients that you can use over multiple meals. Staples such as all-purpose flour and sugar (and baking powder and soda if you're a baker), as well as rice and any other grains you prefer should have a place on your pantry shelves. As for condiments, herbs, and spices, it's best to buy them only as needed, although there are quite a few you are likely to use often, such as olive oil, red or white wine vinegar, salt, and ground black pepper.

Thinking Cold Storage

Refrigerator basics should always include milk, butter, eggs, and cheese. If you're dairy-free, you'll likely want to have plenty of your favorite nut milk on hand. Purchase greens, fruits, and vegetables when they're fresh and only as needed. Choose those that are in season for the best flavor and price. Greens are best stored in the produce drawer, where they are protected from cold temperatures and excess humidity. Many fruits and most vegetables can be kept at cool room temperature, requiring refrigeration only when they begin to overripen. If you have a freezer, buy meats and vegetables in bulk for cost efficiency, then repackage them in individual portions to thaw as needed.

RECIPE SYMBOLS

Once all the basic tools are in hand, it's time to get started. Use this quick key to the recipe symbols as a guide when deciding what to cook.

vegetarian   vegan   gluten-free   microwave   make ahead

BREAKFAST

AÇAI SMOOTHIE BOWL

Açai berries are loaded with plant compounds that act as powerful antioxidants that have been found to benefit the brain, heart, and overall health. With plenty of healthy fats and fiber too, they are an especially good fuel to start the day.

1 In a blender, combine the berry purée, frozen raspberries, and coconut water and blend until smooth.

2 Divide the smoothie between 2 shallow bowls. Arrange the banana, mango, and kiwi decoratively on top. Sprinkle with the granola (if using), goji berries, and coconut, drizzle with the honey, and serve.

prep time: 7 minutes

4 packets (3 oz each) frozen açai berry purée

¼ cup frozen raspberries

½ cup coconut water
or apple juice

1 banana, sliced

1 mango, pitted, peeled,
and sliced

2 kiwifruit, peeled and sliced,
or 6 strawberries, hulled
and sliced

⅓ cup Awesome Granola
(page 16) or store-bought
granola (optional)

2 Tbsp dried goji berries

2 Tbsp unsweetened
shredded coconut

1 Tbsp honey

HACK **KEEP BANANAS FRESH**

To slow the banana ripening process, wrap the stems in plastic wrap to prevent ethylene gas, which naturally occurs during the ripening process, from reaching other parts of the fruit. Store at room temperature.

CHIA PUDDING OVERNIGHT JARS

Chia seeds are tiny whole grains that carry a big nutritional punch. Soaked in milk, juice, or other liquid, they plump to a viscous pudding. You can mix up extra pudding bases to store in the fridge, then top them before heading out the door.

1 Use 2 pint-size jars. In each jar, stir together ¼ cup milk, 1 Tbsp chia seeds, 1½ tsp maple syrup, and 1 dash vanilla. Cover and refrigerate for at least 4 hours or overnight.

2 Stir the chia mixture and set aside at room temperature until the seeds are plumped, about 10 minutes, then layer 1 cup fruit on top of each. Sprinkle each jar with 1 Tbsp coconut chips. Use a long spoon to dig right in, or screw the lid onto each jar for a breakfast to go.

prep time: 5 minutes, plus 4 hours to set

½ cup nut milk, coconut milk, soy milk, or dairy milk

2 Tbsp chia seeds

3 tsp maple syrup

2 dashes pure vanilla extract

2 cups diced mango, whole blueberries, or sliced strawberries, or a combination

2 Tbsp toasted coconut chips

PREPARATION TIP

To dice a mango, cut through the mango just to the side of the center, slicing alongside the large flat pit. Cut off the second side. Using the tip of the knife, cut a grid into the mango flesh without cutting through the skin, then cut along the inside of the mango close to the skin to release the diced flesh.

OATMEAL OVERNIGHT JARS

Once you get the hang of the basic method, you can use nearly any combination of fruits, nuts, spices, and milks for these easy oatmeal jars. A dollop of plain yogurt or applesauce spooned on right before serving can make a nice addition.

1 Use 2 pint-size jars. Put ½ cup oats in each jar, then pour in 1 cup milk. Sprinkle in ½ tsp cinnamon, then layer 2 Tbsp fruit and 2 Tbsp nuts over the top of each. Screw the lid on each jar and refrigerate for at least 4 hours or up to 3 days.

2 Enjoy chilled, or remove the lid, cover loosely with a paper towel, and microwave on high for 1 minute to enjoy warm. Drizzle honey over the top and stir well before eating.

**prep time: 5 minutes,
plus 4 hours to set**

1 cup old-fashioned rolled oats

2 cups dairy milk, nut milk, coconut milk, or soy milk

1 tsp ground cinnamon

4 Tbsp chopped dried peaches or apricots, or whole fresh blackberries or blueberries, or a combination

4 Tbsp chopped toasted pecans, walnuts, or hazelnuts

2–4 tsp honey or other sweetener

COOKING TIP

To toast nuts, preheat an oven to 350ºF. Spread nuts in a single layer on a baking sheet and toast in the oven until lightly browned, about 5 minutes.

AWESOME GRANOLA

Homemade granola always tastes better than store-bought varieties, and you can add whatever you like to customize it. Start with this easy recipe, then swap in your own favorite nuts, seeds, and dried fruits—walnuts or almonds, sunflower or sesame seeds, dried blueberries or cherries—in place of what's here.

1 Preheat the oven to 350°F. Line a rimmed baking sheet with parchment paper.

2 In a large bowl, combine the oats, pecans, coconut, pepitas, sugar, cinnamon, and salt and stir to mix well. In a small bowl or cup, whisk together the oil and vanilla. In another small bowl, beat the egg white with a fork until frothy. Pour the oil mixture over the oat mixture and stir to coat evenly. Then pour the egg white over the oat mixture and stir gently until evenly mixed.

3 Pour the mixture onto the prepared baking sheet, spreading it evenly over the entire surface. Bake the granola, carefully removing the pan from the oven to stir once or twice during baking, until the mixture is nicely toasted, about 35 minutes.

4 Remove from the oven and let cool. Stir in the dried fruit just before serving or storing. Store in an airtight container at room temperature for up to 1 month.

prep time: 10 minutes
cooking time: 35 minutes

2½ cups old-fashioned rolled oats

1 cup chopped pecans

½ cup unsweetened flaked coconut

½ cup pepitas (pumpkin seeds)

⅓ cup firmly packed golden brown sugar

¾ tsp ground cinnamon

¾ tsp salt

½ cup coconut oil or canola oil

1 tsp pure vanilla extract

1 large egg white

⅔ cup dried cranberries or golden raisins, or ⅓ cup each

HACK **RESCUE ROCK-HARD BROWN SUGAR**

To soften brown sugar that has become hard during storage, put it in a microwave-safe container, cover with a damp paper towel, and microwave on high in 20-second intervals until softened.

MILE-HIGH DUTCH BABY

Since it rises so dramatically in the oven, the puffed oven pancake known as a Dutch baby looks a lot harder to make than it is. The simple batter bakes up to a buttery, popover-like shell that makes a delicious "bowl" for sliced fresh fruit.

1 Place a 12-inch oven-safe frying pan in the oven and preheat the oven to 425°F.

2 To make the batter, in a blender, combine the eggs, milk, flour, and salt and blend until smooth. With the motor running, drizzle in 1 Tbsp of the melted butter and blend until incorporated.

3 Put the remaining 1 Tbsp butter in the hot frying pan. Using a pastry brush, carefully brush the butter all over the pan bottom and sides and pour in the batter.

Immediately return the pan to the oven and bake until the Dutch baby is puffed and golden, 15–20 minutes.

4 Meanwhile, make the filling: In a bowl, mix the peaches with the sugar and lemon juice. Let stand until juicy, 10–20 minutes.

5 Remove the pan from the oven. Pour the peaches onto the pancake. Sprinkle with the almonds and dust lightly with powdered sugar (if using). Cut into wedges and serve.

prep time: 5 minutes
cooking time: 20 minutes

FOR THE BATTER

3 large eggs

⅔ cup whole milk

⅔ cup all-purpose flour

¼ tsp salt

2 Tbsp unsalted butter, melted

FOR THE FILLING

2 peaches, peeled, halved, pitted, and sliced

2 tsp sugar

1 Tbsp lemon juice

¼ cup toasted sliced almonds or other nuts

Powdered sugar for dusting (optional)

VARIATION

Brown Butter & Caramelized Apple
Do not put the frying pan in the oven while preheating. Prepare the batter as directed, adding ½ tsp ground cinnamon; set aside. Peel and core 2 apples and cut into wedges. In the frying pan, melt 3 Tbsp butter over medium-high heat. Add the apples and cook, turning as needed, until golden on all sides, about 5 minutes. Add an additional 1 Tbsp butter and heat until bubbling. Pour the batter over the apples, immediately transfer the pan to the oven, and bake as directed. Dust with powdered sugar. Serve with maple syrup.

WHOLE-GRAIN BERRY MUFFINS

This recipe yields a dozen muffins, so you'll have plenty for future breakfasts on the go. Wrap them individually in aluminum foil, seal tightly, and freeze for up to 1 month. To serve, reheat, still wrapped, in a 300°F oven for about 20 minutes.

1 Preheat the oven to 400°F. Line a 12-cup standard muffin pan with paper liners.

2 Process the oats in a food processor or blender until finely ground. Transfer to a bowl and add the flours, sugar, baking powder, baking soda, and salt. Whisk lightly to mix well. In a small bowl, whisk together the buttermilk, oil, and egg. Add the buttermilk mixture to the flour mixture and stir until blended. Gently stir in the berries.

3 To make the streusel, in another small bowl, mix the pecans, sugar, and butter. Using a fork or your fingers, rub lightly until evenly blended.

4 Spoon the batter evenly into the prepared muffin cups. Sprinkle evenly with the streusel. Bake until a toothpick inserted into the center of a muffin comes out clean, about 22 minutes. Let cool in the pan on a wire rack for 5 minutes, then invert onto the rack, turn upright, and let cool completely.

prep time: 8 minutes
cooking time: 22 minutes

---

1 cup old-fashioned rolled oats

¾ cup all-purpose flour

¾ cup whole wheat flour

⅓ cup firmly packed brown sugar

2 tsp baking powder

½ tsp baking soda

½ tsp salt

1¼ cups low-fat buttermilk

2 Tbsp canola oil

1 large egg

1 pint fresh blueberries or raspberries (about 2 cups)

FOR THE STREUSEL

½ cup chopped pecans

2 tsp firmly packed brown sugar

2 tsp unsalted butter, at room temperature

CLASSIC FRENCH TOAST

The secret to extra-good French toast is to use day-old bread—the drier the bread, the more it will absorb the egg mixture. Use bread slices about ¾ inch thick for the best results, and add vanilla extract to the egg mixture for greater depth of flavor.

1 In a baking dish, whisk together the eggs, milk, vanilla, and cinnamon. Add the bread slices, turn to coat, and let soak for 10 minutes, flipping halfway through.

2 In a large frying pan, melt the butter over medium heat.

Working in batches if necessary, add the bread slices and cook, turning once, until golden brown, about 3 minutes per side. Transfer to a serving plate and dust with powdered sugar. Serve with fresh fruit and/or maple syrup to add at the table.

prep time: 15 minutes
cooking time: 6 minutes

3 large eggs

¾ cup whole milk or half-and-half

1½ tsp pure vanilla extract

¼ tsp ground cinnamon

4 slices day-old bread, about ¾ inch thick

1 Tbsp unsalted butter

Powdered sugar for dusting

Fresh sliced fruit and/or maple syrup, warmed, for serving

VARIATIONS

Nut-Crusted
Soak the bread slices in the egg mixture as directed. Spread ½ cup sliced almonds or chopped pecans on a plate. Before frying, dip each bread slice into the nuts, turning to coat both sides and pressing gently on the nuts so they adhere to the bread. Cook as directed.

Jam-Stuffed
Use ½-inch-thick slices of bread. Spread 2–3 tsp jam on each of 2 slices. Cover each with a second slice, press the slices together firmly, and soak as directed, turning to coat the "sandwiches" evenly. Cook as directed, pressing gently on the sandwiches with the back of a spatula and turning carefully.

Pumpkin Pie
Make the egg mixture as directed, but reduce the ¾ cup milk to ½ cup and add ¼ cup canned pumpkin purée. Swap out the ¼ tsp cinnamon for ½ tsp pumpkin pie spice. Cook as directed, about 5 minutes per side. Serve with maple syrup, sweetened whipped cream, and a sprinkle of chopped walnuts or pecans.

ONE-BOWL BANANA BREAD

This quick bread is a great way to use up bananas that have become overripe on your kitchen counter or have been snapped up at the market for a deal, because overly soft bananas with big brown spots are choice for the moistest, most flavorful bread. Cut a slice each morning for a quick, portable breakfast.

1 Preheat the oven to 350°F. Butter a 9 x 5 x 3–inch loaf pan, then dust with flour, tapping out the excess.

2 In a large bowl, mash the bananas with a fork. Add the melted butter, eggs, yogurt, and vanilla. Stir until blended. Add the flour, sugar, baking soda, and salt. Gradually add the flour mixture to the banana mixture, stirring gently just until combined. Stir in the walnuts, if using. Scrape the batter into the prepared pan.

3 Bake until a toothpick inserted into the center comes out clean, about 1 hour. If the top begins to brown too much during baking, cover loosely with aluminum foil. Let the pan cool on a wire rack for 10 minutes, then turn the bread out onto the rack, turn right side up, and let cool completely. Cut the bread into slices and serve. Wrap any leftover bread in plastic wrap and store at room temperature for up to 5 days.

prep time: 10 minutes
cooking time: 1 hour

3 very ripe bananas

½ cup (1 stick) unsalted butter, melted, plus more for greasing

2 large eggs, lightly beaten

⅓ cup plain yogurt

1 tsp pure vanilla extract

2¼ cups all-purpose flour, plus more for dusting

1 cup sugar

1 tsp baking soda

½ tsp salt

1 cup chopped walnuts (optional)

HACK **RIPEN BANANAS IN A HURRY**

To ripen bananas quickly for baking, place them on a baking sheet and bake in a 300°F oven until black and smooth on the outside and soft on the inside, about 40 minutes.

PUMPKIN BREAD FOR A CROWD

This recipe makes 2 loaves—enough to share with all your friends or for 2 weeks' worth of breakfasts. The pumpkin breads will keep, well wrapped, at room temperature for up to 5 days. For longer storage, refrigerate the wrapped loaves for up to 10 days or freeze for up to 1 month and thaw before serving.

1 Preheat the oven to 350°F. Grease two 9 x 5 x 3–inch loaf pans, then dust with flour, tapping out the excess.

2 In a bowl, whisk together the flour, baking soda, salt, baking powder, cinnamon, cloves, and nutmeg. In a large bowl, combine the pumpkin, sugar, oil, eggs, and vanilla and stir until well mixed. Stir in the flour mixture just until blended.

3 Divide the batter evenly between the prepared pans. If desired, sprinkle the walnuts evenly over the tops.

4 Bake until the tops are lightly browned and a toothpick inserted into the center of each loaf comes out clean, 50–55 minutes. If the tops begin to brown too much during baking, cover loosely with aluminum foil. Let the pans cool on a wire rack for 10 minutes, then turn the breads out onto the rack, turn right side up, and let cool completely. Cut each loaf into slices to serve.

prep time: 10 minutes
cooking time: 50 minutes

3 cups all-purpose flour, plus more for dusting

1½ tsp baking soda

1½ tsp salt

1 tsp baking powder

1 tsp ground cinnamon

1 tsp ground cloves

1 tsp ground nutmeg

1 can (15 oz) pumpkin purée

3 cups sugar

1 cup canola oil, plus more for greasing

3 large eggs

1 tsp pure vanilla extract

½ cup chopped walnuts (optional)

FRUIT SMOOTHIES

A decent blender may just be the one basic appliance you can't do without in a college kitchen—especially once you discover a favorite smoothie to start the day. Try any of these ideas, subbing in your own favorite ingredients, if you like.

GREEN ENERGY In a blender, combine 3–4 ice cubes, 1 banana, 1 cup *each* frozen mango cubes and fresh spinach leaves, ½ cup coconut water, 1 tsp chia seeds, and 1 dash pure vanilla extract. Blend until smooth, then divide between 2 glasses. Sprinkle with extra chia seeds before serving.

LAVA FLOW In a glass measuring pitcher or small bowl, combine 1 cup hulled, chopped strawberries with 2 Tbsp sugar and mash with a fork; set aside. In a blender, combine 6 ice cubes, 1 banana, ¾ cup pineapple juice, ½ cup milk, and 1½ Tbsp coconut cream. Blend until smooth, then divide between 2 glasses. Pour an equal amount of the strawberry mixture into each glass, adding it in a single overflowing gush.

BERRY BLAST In a blender, combine 3–4 ice cubes, 1½ cups fresh or frozen mixed berries, and ½ cup *each* red grapes, vanilla Greek yogurt, and coconut water or berry juice. Blend until smooth, then divide between 2 glasses. Sprinkle with extra berries before serving.

MATCHA MANGO In a blender, combine 3–4 ice cubes, 1 banana, 2 cups frozen mango cubes, and ½ cup *each* vanilla Greek yogurt and orange juice. Blend until smooth, then divide between 2 glasses. Sprinkle about 1 tsp matcha green tea powder over the smoothies before serving, dividing it evenly.

PERFECT EGGS THREE WAYS

Understanding the basics of egg prep could just be one of the most important cooking lessons of your college career. And it's not an exacting science. Cooking eggs to perfection can have as much to do with personal preference as it can with technique. Learn these tried-and-true methods, then modify them to suit your taste.

Boiled

cooking time: 4–8 minutes

Bring a saucepan of water to a boil over high heat. Using a slotted spoon, gently lower 1 or more eggs into the water. Reduce the heat to low and simmer for 4 minutes for eggs with soft, runny yolks, 6 minutes for medium-firm yolks, and 8 minutes for firm yolks. Drain. For medium- or hard-cooked eggs, rinse under cold running water or transfer to an ice bath until cool. When the eggs are cool, crack and peel them or refrigerate for later.

Fried

cooking time: 2–3 minutes

To prepare sunny-side-up eggs, in a large frying pan, preferably nonstick, heat 1–2 tsp olive oil or unsalted butter per large egg over medium heat. Crack the egg(s) into the pan, cooking only as many as will comfortably fit in the pan. Season with salt and pepper and cook until the whites are opaque and the yolks thicken, 2–3 minutes. Serve.

To prepare over-easy, over-medium, or over-hard eggs, cook as directed above for sunny side up, then carefully flip the egg(s) with a nonstick spatula and cook for about 30 seconds longer for eggs over easy, about 1 minute longer for eggs over medium, and about 1½ minutes longer for eggs over hard. Serve.

Poached

cooking time: 2–4 minutes

Pour water into a large saucepan to a depth of 2 inches. Bring to a gentle simmer over medium-low heat. One at a time, crack the eggs into a ramekin or a small cup and gently slide them into the simmering water. Cook as many eggs at a time as will comfortably fit in the pan. Cook until the whites begin to set, about 2 minutes, then gently turn the eggs with a slotted spoon. Continue to cook until the whites are opaque and fully cooked and the yolks are still runny, about 2 minutes longer. Using the slotted spoon, lift each egg from the simmering water, draining well. Blot the bottom of each egg briefly on a paper towel, then serve.

PERFECT SCRAMBLED EGGS

The best method for preparing scrambled eggs is a topic of some debate, but most chefs (especially the French ones) agree that slow-cooking beaten eggs over low heat results in an ideal custardy texture. Serve them plain, or revved up with bell peppers, sausage, and cheese. Or ditch the stove and scramble eggs in a microwave.

1 In a bowl, whisk together the eggs and milk and season with salt and pepper.

2 In a large nonstick frying pan, melt the butter over medium-low heat. Pour in the egg mixture and cook without stirring for 1 minute. Using a rubber spatula, gently stir the eggs, allowing the uncooked eggs to run to the bottom of the pan. Cook, stirring often, until the eggs are set but still creamy, about 4 minutes. Transfer to a plate and serve.

prep time: 1 minute
cooking time: 5 minutes

2 large eggs
1½ tsp milk
Salt and pepper
1 tsp unsalted butter

VARIATION

Bell Pepper, Sausage & Jack
Prepare the egg mixture as directed above. In a large nonstick frying pan, heat 2 tsp olive oil over medium-high heat. Add ¼ bell pepper, seeded and sliced, and 1 oz sliced andouille sausage and cook until the sausage is browned, about 5 minutes. Reduce the heat to medium-low. Add the egg mixture and cook as directed above until mostly set, about 3 minutes. Stir in 1 Tbsp shredded Monterey jack cheese and 1 tsp sliced green onion. Continue to gently stir until the eggs are set, about 1 minute longer, then serve.

MICROWAVE IT
Coat a microwave-safe bowl or large mug with cooking spray. Add 2 large eggs and 2 Tbsp milk and whisk until blended, then season with salt and pepper. Microwave on high for 45 seconds, stir gently, then continue to microwave until the eggs are nearly set, 30–45 seconds longer. (They will continue to firm up after they are removed from the microwave.) Serve.

BACON, EGG & SPINACH MUFFIN CUPS

Bake these easy egg cups on a Sunday and you'll have enough to last you for the whole week. Refrigerate the leftover cups, then reheat in the microwave. For a lighter version, use turkey bacon and swap in purchased egg whites for half of the eggs.

1 Preheat the oven to 375°F. Coat the 12 cups of a standard muffin pan with cooking spray.

2 Rinse the frozen spinach in a colander with cold running water for 10–20 seconds, then let it thaw while you cook the bacon.

3 In a frying pan, fry the bacon over medium heat, stirring often, until lightly browned on the edges, 3–4 minutes. Transfer the bacon to a paper towel–lined plate and pour off all but 1 Tbsp of the bacon fat in the pan. Return the pan to low heat, add the green onion, and cook, stirring, for 1 minute. Add the onion to the plate with the bacon.

4 In a bowl, whisk the eggs and milk until blended. Squeeze the spinach dry with your hands and add to the egg mixture. Add the cheese, bacon, and green onion. Stir gently until mixed.

5 Pour the egg mixture into the prepared muffin cups. Bake until the eggs are puffy and set, 20–22 minutes. Serve warm or at room temperature.

prep time: 10 minutes
cooking time: 20 minutes

¼ package (2½ oz) frozen spinach leaves or 1 cup loose frozen leaves

4 bacon strips, thinly sliced crosswise

2 Tbsp thinly sliced green onion

8 large eggs

4 Tbsp milk

¾ cup shredded Monterey jack cheese

EASY CHEESY EGG BAKE

If you time this right, you can put an egg in the oven, shower, then eat just before heading out the door. A tomato or mushroom shell is a nice alternative to the dish.

1 Preheat the oven to 300°F. Grease a small baking dish or ramekin.

2 Sprinkle half of the cheese in the prepared baking dish. Crack the egg on top of the cheese. Scatter the crumbled bacon over the egg, then cover with the remaining cheese.

Season with salt and pepper and sprinkle with the bread crumbs.

3 Bake until the egg white is set and the yolk has begun to thicken but is still a bit runny, about 15 minutes. The bread crumbs should be lightly browned; if they're not, slide the dish under the hot broiler for 1 or 2 minutes. Serve hot.

prep time: 5 minutes
cooking time: 15 minutes

½ cup coarsely shredded cheese such as Gruyère

1 large egg

1 bacon strip, cooked and crumbled

Salt and pepper

1 Tbsp fresh bread crumbs

VARIATIONS

Tomato Egg Bake
Preheat the oven to 450°F. Line a rimmed baking sheet with aluminum foil. Cut off the top one-fourth of 1 medium tomato. Using a spoon, hollow out the tomato, leaving a cup about ½ inch thick. Place the tomato cup on the prepared baking sheet and sprinkle the inside with salt and pepper. Crack 1 large egg into the tomato and sprinkle with 1 Tbsp grated Parmesan cheese. Bake until the egg white is set and the yolk has begun to thicken but is still a bit runny, 8–10 minutes, then serve.

Portobello Mushroom Egg Bake
Preheat the oven to 425°F. Remove the stem and gills from 1 portobello mushroom. Place the mushroom cap, stemmed side up, on a rimmed baking sheet and spray with cooking spray or brush lightly with olive oil. Sprinkle ½ tomato, diced, 1 Tbsp diced ham, and 1 tsp thinly sliced green onion into the mushroom cap, then crack 1 large egg on top. Bake until the egg white is set and the yolk has begun to thicken but is still a bit runny, about 10 minutes, then serve.

ULTIMATE MICROWAVE BREAKFAST

The only element missing from this mug breakfast is a few pieces of crisp bacon (page 123), which also cook up quickly in the microwave.

Cheesy Scrambled Eggs in a Mug

1 Coat a microwave-safe mug or bowl with cooking spray. Add the eggs and milk and whisk until blended. Stir in the cheese, bacon, and onion, and season with salt and pepper.

2 Microwave on high for 45 seconds, stir gently, then continue to microwave until the eggs are nearly set, 30–45 seconds longer. (They will continue to firm up after they are removed from the microwave.) Serve warm.

prep time: 1 minute
cooking time: 1½ minutes

Cooking spray

2 large eggs

2 Tbsp milk

2 Tbsp shredded cheese such as Cheddar or Monterey jack

2 Tbsp diced cooked bacon

1 tsp thinly sliced green onion

Salt and pepper

Mug Coffee Cake

1 In a mug, mix the butter and sugar until well blended. Stir in the sour cream and egg until evenly mixed, then stir in the flour and baking powder. Sprinkle with the cinnamon and the raisins (if using).

2 Microwave on high for 1 minute, then leave the cake in the microwave with the door closed for 1 minute to steam and cool. The cake should be moist but cooked throughout. Serve warm.

prep time: 1 minute
cooking time: 2 minutes

1 Tbsp unsalted butter, at room temperature

2 Tbsp *each* sugar and sour cream or plain Greek yogurt

1 Tbsp beaten egg

¼ cup all-purpose flour

⅛ tsp *each* baking powder and ground cinnamon

1 tsp raisins (optional)

FRIED EGG BREAKFAST SANDWICHES

Add a fried egg to just about any favorite sandwich and it becomes a tasty way to start the day. Prepare the sandwich ingredients first, then fry up the egg according to your liking and add it just before serving. Use the very best bread your budget will allow, and season liberally with salt and pepper before you take a bite.

Breakfast Bánh Mì

1 In a nonaluminum bowl, combine the carrot, onion, vinegar, sugar, and salt and stir to combine. Set aside at room temperature for at least 20 minutes or up to 2 hours, or cover and refrigerate for up to 5 days.

2 Drain the pickled vegetables and stir in the cilantro and

mint. Spread the cut sides of the baguette pieces with the Sriracha mayonnaise. Add the bacon, pickled vegetables, and fried egg to the bottom half of the baguette piece. Cover with the top half and serve.

prep time: 10 minutes, plus 20 minutes to pickle

¼ carrot, shredded

2 thin slices red onion, separated into rings

1 Tbsp rice vinegar

½ tsp sugar

⅛ tsp salt

1 Tbsp fresh cilantro leaves, coarsely chopped

4 fresh mint leaves, coarsely chopped

¼ baguette, cut into 2 sandwich halves

2 Tbsp mayonnaise mixed with 2 tsp Sriracha and 1 tsp lemon juice

2 slices thick-cut cooked bacon (page 123)

1 Fried Egg (page 26)

HACK **REVIVE STALE BREAD**

To refresh a stale baguette, rinse it liberally in running water, then enclose the wet loaf in aluminum foil. Place in a preheated 300°F oven and bake until softened, about 10 minutes. Remove the foil, return the baguette to the oven, and continue to bake until crisp on the outside and soft in the center, 4–5 minutes longer.

Continued on page 34

Continued from page 33

Grilled Cheese Sandwich with Bacon, Tomato, Avocado & Egg

1 Place one slice of cheese on one slice of bread, then layer on the bacon, egg, avocado, tomato, and second slice of cheese. Top with the remaining bread slice, pressing firmly. Spread the butter evenly over the top and bottom bread slices.

2 Heat a frying pan over medium heat or heat a panini press if you have one. Add the sandwich to the pan and press firmly with the back of a spatula, or slip the sandwich into the press and close the top. Cook, turning once in the pan and pressing gently, until golden brown on both sides, about 4 minutes total. Transfer the sandwich to a cutting board, cut in half, and serve hot.

prep time: 5 minutes
cooking time: 5 minutes

2 slices cheese, such as mozzarella, provolone, Monterey jack, or Cheddar

2 slices bread, such as whole grain, sourdough, or coarse country bread

2 slices cooked bacon (page 123), cut in half

1 Fried Egg (page 26)

¼ avocado, peeled and sliced

2–3 slices tomato, drained on paper towels

Unsalted butter for spreading

Breakfast Cubano

1 Spread mustard on both bread slices. Place a slice of cheese (folded in half if necessary) on one bread slice. Add the ham on top of the cheese, then add half of the pickle spears. Place the fried egg on top of the pickles, add the remaining pickles on top of the egg, and then add the remaining slice of cheese (folded in half if necessary). Close the sandwich with the other bread slice, mustard side down, pressing gently. Spread half of the butter evenly over the top of the sandwich.

2 In a frying pan, melt the remaining butter over medium heat. Add the sandwich, buttered side up, to the pan. Cover and cook, turning once, until golden brown, about 4 minutes per side. Cut the sandwich in half and serve.

prep time: 5 minutes
cooking time: 8 minutes

1 Tbsp yellow mustard

2 slices crusty French or Italian bread, ½ inch thick

2 slices Swiss cheese

2–3 slices ham

½ dill pickle, cut lengthwise into 2–4 spears

1 Fried Egg (page 26)

1 Tbsp unsalted butter, at room temperature

CALIFORNIA OMELET

With a little practice and a high-quality nonstick frying pan, making omelets can become an easy morning ritual. The best fillings start with a good melting cheese, then add in your own favorite ingredients.

1 In a bowl, whisk together the eggs, milk, ⅛ tsp salt, and a pinch of pepper just until blended. In a small nonstick frying pan, melt the butter over medium heat, tilting the pan to cover the bottom evenly. Pour the egg mixture into the pan and cook until the eggs have barely begun to set around the edges, about 30 seconds. Using a heatproof spatula, lift the cooked edges and gently push them toward the center, tilting the pan to allow the liquid egg on top to flow underneath, then cook for 30 seconds longer. Repeat this process, moving around the perimeter of the pan, until no liquid egg remains.

2 When the eggs are almost completely set, sprinkle the cheese over half of the omelet. Scatter the bacon, avocado, salsa, and sprouts over the cheese. Using the spatula, fold the plain half of the omelet over the filled half to create a half-moon shape. Let the omelet cook for 30 seconds longer, then slide it onto a plate and serve.

prep time: 5 minutes
cooking time: 5 minutes

FOR THE OMELET

2 large eggs
1 Tbsp milk
Salt and pepper
1 tsp unsalted butter

FOR THE FILLING

¼ cup shredded cheese such as Cheddar or Monterey jack
1 thick-cut bacon strip, cooked and torn into bite-size pieces
¼ avocado, pitted, peeled, and sliced
2 Tbsp tomato salsa
2 Tbsp alfalfa or sunflower sprouts

VARIATIONS

Mushroom, Cheese & Herb
In a nonstick frying pan, melt 1 tsp unsalted butter over medium heat. Add ¼ cup sliced mushrooms and cook, stirring occasionally, until the mushrooms begin to brown, about 6 minutes. Stir in ¼ tsp chopped fresh thyme or parsley and season with salt and pepper. Transfer to a bowl and set aside, along with ¼ cup shredded fontina cheese. Whisk the egg mixture and cook the omelet as directed above, adding the cheese, then the mushroom filling.

Ham, Tomato & Cheese
Set aside 2 slices deli ham and 1 small tomato, sliced, for the filling, along with ¼ cup shredded cheese. Whisk the egg mixture and cook the omelet as directed above, adding the cheese, then the ham and tomato.

SOUPS & SALADS

BUTTERNUT SQUASH & APPLE SOUP

This soup is a good one to stretch into easy bowls for the week. Vary it by adding a different garnish every time. Try buttery croutons (as here), a swirl of Greek yogurt, a sprinkling of chili powder and salted pepitas, or a scattering of sliced almonds.

1 In a large saucepan, melt the butter over medium heat. Add the onion and cook, stirring, until tender, about 8 minutes. Stir in the garlic and cook for 1 minute. Add the squash, apples, and 5 cups broth, cover, and simmer until the squash is very tender, about 20 minutes.

2 Remove from the heat and let cool slightly. Purée the soup using an immersion blender in the pot, or transfer the soup in batches to a regular blender. (If using a regular blender, let the squash mixture cool to lukewarm before blending and allow steam to escape from the blender by removing the center plug from the blender lid while puréeing.) Add more broth, if needed, for the desired consistency.

3 Season the soup to taste with salt and pepper. Ladle into bowls and serve.

prep time: 15 minutes
cooking time: 35 minutes

---

2 Tbsp unsalted butter

1 yellow onion, halved and sliced

2 garlic cloves, minced or pressed

1 butternut squash (about 4 lb), halved, seeded, peeled, and cut into chunks

2 apples, peeled, cored, and cut into chunks

5–6 cups vegetable broth or reduced-sodium chicken broth

Salt and pepper

HACK **CUT HARD SQUASH WITH EASE**

To make butternut squash easier to peel and cut, microwave it first. Use a fork to poke holes all over the squash, then cut a 1-inch slice from the top and bottom. Microwave on high for 3½ minutes. When the squash is cool enough to handle, use a vegetable peeler to remove the peel, then cut with a knife and remove the seeds before using.

WHITE BEAN SOUP WITH PARMESAN

This classic soup begins with *mirepoix* (a mix of chopped onion, carrot, and celery) which creates a tasty base for just about any soup or sauce. Mashing half of the beans enhances its thick texture, but you can skip that step if you're in a hurry. For extra flavor, add diced ham or chopped chard leaves with the Parmesan.

1 In a large saucepan, warm the oil over medium heat. Add the onion, carrot, and celery and cook, stirring occasionally, until the vegetables are soft, about 10 minutes. Stir in the garlic and thyme and cook for 3 minutes longer. Add the beans and broth and bring to a boil. Reduce the heat to low and simmer gently until the vegetables are tender, about 15 minutes.

2 Remove from the heat. Transfer about one-third of the soup to a bowl. Using an immersion blender, a fork, or a potato masher, mash the beans until mostly smooth, then stir the mixture back into the soup.

3 Stir the Parmesan into the soup, then season to taste with salt and pepper. Serve with more Parmesan for adding at the table.

prep time: 10 minutes
cooking time: 30 minutes

2 Tbsp olive oil

1 yellow onion, finely chopped

1 carrot, peeled and finely chopped

1 rib celery, finely chopped

2 cloves garlic, minced

¼ tsp dried thyme or rosemary

2 cans (15 oz each) reduced-sodium cannellini or white kidney beans, drained and rinsed

6 cups vegetable broth or reduced-sodium chicken broth

¼ cup grated Parmesan cheese, plus more for serving

Salt and pepper

COOKING TIP

If the Parmesan rind is left over from the cheese after grating, add the rind to the soup while it's simmering for extra flavor.

CHICKEN-TORTILLA SOUP

With some cooked chicken on hand (whether homemade or purchased), this popular soup can be ready in under 20 minutes. Add some chopped tomato or canned black beans for a chunkier texture. If making the soup ahead, don't add the chips, cheese, avocado, or cilantro until just before serving.

1 In a large saucepan, warm the oil over medium heat. Add the onion and cook, stirring, until translucent, about 3 minutes. Add the chili powder and stir until fragrant, about 1 minute. Pour in the broth and bring to a boil. Add the shredded chicken and simmer until the chicken is heated through, about 3 minutes.

2 Add the lime juice and salt to taste. Ladle into bowls and serve, allowing diners to garnish their bowls as desired with the tortilla chips, queso fresco, avocado, and cilantro.

prep time: 10 minutes
cooking time: 10 minutes

1 Tbsp olive oil

½ yellow onion, finely chopped

2 tsp chili powder

6 cups reduced-sodium chicken broth

2 cups shredded Cooked Chicken (page 123)

Juice of 3–4 limes

Salt

1½ cups broken tortilla chips

½ cup crumbled queso fresco or shredded Monterey jack cheese

1 Hass avocado, pitted, peeled, and cubed

¼ cup chopped fresh cilantro

PREPARATION TIP

To dice an avocado like a pro, cut into the center of an avocado, cutting all the way around the big round pit. Separate the avocado halves. Remove the pit by whacking it with a chef's knife, then twisting gently. Use the tip of the knife to cut a grid into the flesh without cutting through the skin, then slip a spoon between the flesh and skin to scoop out the cubes.

RAMEN UPGRADE

With a few expert add-ins and a touch of whimsy, your spiffed-up store-bought ramen can be every bit as good as the food truck or ramen joint variety. The requisite boiling water cooks some of the last-minute ingredients in the bowl, while others are best added just before serving.

ADD TO DRY NOODLES BEFORE ADDING BOILING WATER

- Very thinly sliced pork or beef tenderloin (It will cook in the boiling water.)
- Peeled and grated fresh ginger
- Thinly sliced green onion
- Frozen or fresh spinach leaves
- Frozen or fresh peas
- Frozen or fresh edamame

ADD TO THE BOWL JUST BEFORE SERVING

- Roasted cherry tomatoes
  Toss tomatoes with a drizzle of olive oil. Roast in a 450°F oven for 10 minutes.
- Roasted root vegetables (page 75)
- Chopped fresh herbs
- Soft-boiled egg (page 26), halved
- Thinly sliced radish
- Chili powder or dried red chile flakes

Making Faux Pho

Faking an authentic bowl of Vietnamese pho from standard supermarket ramen is easy with the addition of spice-steeped broth and traditional ingredients.

1. In a tea ball or muslin spice bag, mix 1 tsp coriander seeds, ½ cinnamon stick, 1 whole clove, and 1 pinch anise seeds.

2. Add the tea ball to the dry ramen noodles along with the spice packet seasonings, 1 knob peeled fresh ginger, 1 tsp fish sauce, ½ tsp sugar, and 2 oz very thinly sliced pork tenderloin. Add the boiling water and steep according to the package directions.

3. Remove the tea ball. Transfer the soup to a serving bowl. Add fresh cilantro or basil leaves, thinly sliced red onion and red chile, mung bean sprouts, and a lime wedge. Add Sriracha to taste at the table.

CHINESE CHICKEN SALAD WITH SESAME-LIME VINAIGRETTE

Keep this classic mix simple, or bulk it up with any of your favorite additions. Use store-bought or homemade roast (page 94) or poached (page 123) chicken, or add a more rustic flavor by grilling up a chicken breast to add instead.

1 To make the vinaigrette, combine all the ingredients in a small jar with lid, cover and shake vigorously.

2 To make the salad, in a large serving bowl, combine the cabbage, chicken, green onions, almonds, salt, and pepper. Add 1 Tbsp of the cilantro plus any of the optional add-ins noted below. Drizzle some of the vinaigrette over the salad and toss to coat thoroughly. Taste and and add more vinaigrette if needed. Sprinkle with the remaining 1 Tbsp cilantro and serve.

prep time: 10 minutes

FOR THE SESAME-LIME VINAIGRETTE

⅓ **cup toasted sesame oil**

6 **Tbsp lime juice**

2 **Tbsp seasoned rice vinegar**

1 **Tbsp Dijon mustard**

1 **Tbsp sugar**

¾ **tsp salt**

FOR THE SALAD

½ **head napa cabbage, halved lengthwise, cored, and sliced crosswise**

½ **cup shredded cooked chicken (see note above)**

2 **green onions, including tender green tops, thinly sliced**

2 **Tbsp toasted sliced almonds**

2 **tsp salt, plus more to taste**

1 **tsp pepper, plus more to taste**

2 **Tbsp finely chopped fresh cilantro**

PREPARATION TIP

For added flavor and variety, incorporate your own favorite Asian salad ingredients in this mix. Try sliced bell pepper strips, sliced cucumber, canned mandarin orange slices, mung bean sprouts, and/or crisp chow mein noodles.

CLASSIC CAESAR SALAD WITH GARLIC CROUTONS

A trusted recipe for classic Caesar dressing is a cooking necessity. Homemade croutons may seem like a hassle, but they definitely make a difference. If you're reluctant to use raw egg, substitute 1 cup mayonnaise for the egg, oil, and vinegar.

1 To make the croutons, preheat the oven to 350°F. In a bowl, whisk together the oil and garlic. Add the bread cubes and a pinch of salt and mix well. Spread the pieces in a single layer on a rimmed baking sheet. Toast, stirring occasionally, until the cubes are golden brown, 9–12 minutes. Let cool completely before using.

2 To make the dressing, crack the egg into a small bowl. Add the lemon juice, vinegar, Worcestershire, anchovies, and garlic and whisk to combine well. Gradually whisk in the oil. Stir in the grated Parmesan cheese and season to taste with salt and pepper.

3 To make the salad, in a large bowl, toss the lettuce and croutons with half of the dressing. Taste and add more dressing if desired (you may not use all of it). Divide the salad between 2 plates. Using a vegetable peeler, shave thin curls of Parmesan cheese over each salad and serve.

prep time: 10 minutes
cooking time: 10 minutes

FOR THE GARLIC CROUTONS

2 Tbsp olive oil

1 large clove garlic, minced

¼ loaf day-old country bread, cut into cubes

Salt

FOR THE DRESSING

1 large egg

2 Tbsp lemon juice

1 tsp red wine vinegar

½ tsp Worcestershire sauce

1½ Tbsp minced anchovy fillets

1 small clove garlic, minced

½ cup olive oil

½ cup grated Parmesan cheese

Salt and pepper

FOR THE SALAD

1 romaine lettuce heart (about ½ lb), leaves separated and cut into bite-size pieces

2 oz Parmesan cheese for shaving

VARIATION

Chicken Caesar
Add ½ cup shredded or diced cooked chicken (pages 94 and 123) with the lettuce and croutons.

SUPERFOOD KALE & QUINOA SALAD

A healthy mix of kale and quinoa provides an excellent protein- and fiber-rich building block for any superfood blend. Goji berries and avocado add flavor, as well as a healthful blend of vitamins and nutrients.

1 To make the vinaigrette, in a jar with a lid, combine all the ingredients. Cover and shake until evenly blended. Taste and add more olive oil, salt, or pepper if needed.

2 To make the salad, in a bowl, toss together the kale, quinoa, carrots, mint, nuts, sesame seeds, and goji berries. Just before serving, add the avocado and vinaigrette and toss gently to mix.

prep time: 10 minutes

FOR THE LEMON VINAIGRETTE

2 Tbsp lemon juice

1 Tbsp white wine vinegar

¼ cup olive oil, or to taste

Salt and pepper to taste

FOR THE SALAD

2 cups baby kale or mixed kale and spinach

1 cup Cooked Quinoa (page 122)

2 small carrots, thinly sliced

2 Tbsp fresh mint leaves

2 Tbsp toasted sliced almonds, roasted pepitas, or toasted pecans

1 Tbsp sesame seeds

1 Tbsp goji berries

¼ avocado, peeled and sliced

PREPARATION TIP

The more superfood favorites you incorporate into this salad, the more richly flavored and healthful it becomes. In addition to or in place of any of the ingredients included here, try black beans, roasted sweet potato, hard-boiled egg, broccoli florets, rolled oats, chia seeds, or blue corn.

THAI RICE NOODLE SALAD WITH CHICKEN & SUMMER VEGETABLES

For a shortcut to this tasty Thai-inspired salad, add in purchased rotisserie chicken instead of cooking your own. And if a moment of culinary inspiration leads to the acquisition of a spiralizer, use it to prep the cucumber, carrot, and zucchini here.

1 Preheat the oven to 375°F. Set a wire rack inside a roasting pan.

2 To cook the chicken, pat the chicken thighs dry with paper towels. Brush the chicken lightly on both sides with olive oil, sprinkle with the cumin, and season generously with salt and pepper. Place on the rack in the roasting pan and roast, turning once, until golden brown and opaque at the center, 25–30 minutes. Let cool.

3 Make the Thai vinaigrette, pour into a large bowl, and set aside.

4 To make the salad, prepare the rice noodles according to the package directions, then rinse under cold running water and drain well. Add the noodles to the bowl with the vinaigrette and toss to coat.

5 Pull the chicken meat from the bones and shred it; discard the skin. Add the chicken, cucumber, carrot, zucchini, bell pepper, and green onions to the noodles and toss gently to mix. Before serving, sprinkle with basil and mint, if desired.

prep time: 5 minutes
cooking time: 15 minutes

FOR THE CHICKEN

3 bone-in, skin-on chicken thighs, about 1 lb total

Olive oil for brushing

½ tsp ground cumin

Salt and pepper

THAI VINAIGRETTE
(page 124)

FOR THE SALAD

¼ lb thin dried rice noodles

¼ English cucumber, sliced

1 small carrot, peeled and sliced

½ small zucchini, sliced

½ yellow bell pepper, seeded and thinly sliced

5 green onions, white and pale green parts, thinly sliced

Small fresh basil and mint leaves, for garnish (optional)

HACK KEEP HERBS FRESH

To prolong the life of fresh herbs, place the herbs stem down in a mason jar half filled with water like flowers in a vase. Cover loosely with a plastic bag and store in the refrigerator.

TACO SALAD WITH SALSA VINAIGRETTE

Once you prepare the taco meat for this salad, you should have enough to enjoy all week or to share with your roommates. If you're stretching the ingredients over several meals, don't add the avocado and vinaigrette until just before you eat.

1 To make the vinaigrette, in a small jar with a lid or other covered container, mix the salsa, vinegar, and lime juice. Add 4 Tbsp of the oil, cover, and shake until mixed. Taste and add up to 2 Tbsp more oil if needed. Set aside.

2 To make the salad, cook the ground beef with the taco seasoning and water according to the package directions. (The cooked meat can be cooled, covered, and refrigerated for up to 4 days.)

3 While the meat is cooking, slice the lettuce. For each salad, combine one-quarter each of the lettuce, tomatoes, beans, and avocado, then top with one-quarter each of the meat and cheese. Spoon some of the salsa vinaigrette over each salad. Top with tortilla chips and serve.

prep time: 5 minutes
cooking time: 10 minutes

FOR THE SALSA VINAIGRETTE

1 Tbsp mild salsa

1 Tbsp red wine vinegar

2 tsp lime juice

4–6 Tbsp olive oil

FOR THE SALAD

1 lb ground beef

1 packet (about 1 oz) taco seasoning mix

½ head iceberg lettuce

3 plum tomatoes, diced

1 cup canned black or pinto beans, drained and rinsed

1 avocado, pitted, peeled, and diced

1½ cups shredded Cheddar cheese

Tortilla chips

GREEK-STYLE BEEF SALAD

This salad is enough for a hefty meal on its own. Make it portable by wrapping it up in a warmed pita or other flatbread—preferably one that has been amply smeared with Hummus (page 125). Swap in cooked chicken (page 123) for the beef, if you like.

1 To make the vinaigrette, in a small jar with a lid or other covered container, mix the lemon juice, mint, garlic, salt, and pepper. Add the oil, cover, and shake until mixed. Taste and season with more salt and pepper, if needed.

2 To make the salad, in a large bowl, combine all the ingredients and gently toss to mix. Just before serving, drizzle with some of the vinaigrette and toss to coat, adding more vinaigrette if needed. Divide among individual bowls and serve.

prep time: 5 minutes

FOR THE MINT VINAIGRETTE

Juice of 1 lemon

1 Tbsp chopped fresh mint

1 small clove garlic, minced

1/8 tsp salt, plus more to taste

1/8 tsp ground pepper, plus more to taste

1/4 cup olive oil

FOR THE SALAD

1 small head baby romaine lettuce, separated into leaves

1/2 cup chopped cooked beef tri-tip (page 95) or store-bought sliced roast beef

1/2 red onion, halved lengthwise and thinly sliced crosswise

1/2 cucumber, halved lengthwise, seeded, and thinly sliced crosswise

1/2 cup cherry tomatoes, halved

1/3 cup Kalamata or other Mediterranean black olives, pitted and coarsely chopped

1/2 cup crumbled feta cheese

HACK AVOID ONION TEARS

To prevent onion fumes from causing your eyes to water, try chewing gum or holding a piece of bread in your mouth when cutting an onion.

SNACKS

SPICY BUFFALO WINGS

Make sure you have plenty of napkins on hand when serving these spicy wings, as well as a smooth, bubbly beverage to temper the intense flavor. If you have a grill, retire the oven and grill the wings instead. For an even spicier finish, up the quantity of pepper sauce. Serve with Ranch or Blue Cheese dressing for dipping.

1 In a bowl, stir together the vinegar, oil, Worcestershire, Tabasco, chili powder, red pepper flakes, salt, and black pepper. Reserve ¼ cup of the marinade. Put the chicken wings in a large lock-top plastic bag and pour in the remaining marinade. Press out the air from the bag and seal. Massage the bag gently to distribute the marinade. Set the bag in a large bowl and refrigerate for 2–3 hours, turning and massaging the bag occasionally.

2 Preheat the oven to 450°F. Line 2 baking sheets with aluminum foil and coat with cooking spray. Arrange the wings on the prepared baking sheet, reserving the marinade. Bake, turning once or twice and brushing with the reserved marinade, until opaque throughout when pierced, 20-25 minutes. Serve hot or at room temperature, with dressing if desired.

prep time: 10 minutes, plus 2 hours to marinate

cooking time: 25 minutes

---

1 cup apple cider vinegar

2 Tbsp canola oil

2 Tbsp Worcestershire sauce

1 Tbsp Tabasco or other hot pepper sauce

2 Tbsp chili powder

1 tsp red pepper flakes

1 tsp salt

1 tsp ground black pepper

4 lb chicken wings

Cooking spray

Ranch or Blue Cheese Dressing (page 125) for serving (optional)

COOKING TIP

If grilling, consider using only the larger, meatier section of the wings (often labeled drumettes) instead of whole wings, whose bony tips burn easily on a grill.

FULLY LOADED NACHOS

Nachos are party fare, and this hefty plate is no exception. Sub in your own favorites when it comes to toppings—try shredded chicken for the beef, pintos for the black beans, and pepper jack for the Cheddar.

1 In a frying pan, brown the ground beef over medium-high heat, breaking it up with a wooden spoon, until cooked through, about 5 minutes. Pour off all but about 2 Tbsp fat and place over medium heat. Stir in the chili powder, cumin, and salt and continue to cook for 1 minute. Remove the pan from the heat and set aside.

2 In a saucepan, melt the butter over medium heat. Add the flour and whisk constantly for 1–2 minutes. Slowly whisk in the milk.

When the milk begins to bubble, add the cheese a handful at a time, stirring constantly with a wooden spoon. Remove the cheese sauce from the heat and season to taste with salt.

3 Arrange the tortilla chips in a shallow serving dish. Pour the cheese sauce over the chips and top with the ground beef, black beans, tomatoes, red onion, and jalapeños. Serve with salsa, guacamole, and sour cream on the side.

prep time: 10 minutes
cooking time: 10 minutes

---

1 lb ground beef

1 Tbsp chili powder

1 Tbsp ground cumin

¾ tsp salt, plus more to taste

2 Tbsp unsalted butter

2 Tbsp all-purpose flour

2 cups whole milk

2½ cups (12 oz) shredded Cheddar cheese

1 bag (14 oz) tortilla chips

1 can (15 oz) black beans, drained and rinsed

2 tomatoes, chopped

¼ small red onion, thinly sliced

⅓ cup (2½ oz) sliced jalapeño chiles

Fresh Tomato Salsa, Guacamole (page 124), and sour cream for serving

STICKY SESAME DRUMETTES

Serve these super tasty drumettes to friends or make a batch and store them in a covered container in the fridge, ready to reheat anytime hunger calls. Reducing the sauce thickens it enough to create the perfect sweet, sticky coating.

1 In a large bowl, whisk together the maple syrup, soy sauce, ginger, garlic, and pepper. Add the chicken drumettes to the bowl and toss to coat well. Cover and marinate in the refrigerator for at least 1 hour and up to overnight, tossing the drumettes a few times in the marinade.

2 Preheat the oven to 375°F. Coat a rimmed baking sheet lightly with cooking spray, line it with aluminum foil, and coat again.

3 Remove the drumettes from the marinade, reserving the marinade, and arrange them in a single layer on the prepared baking sheet. Bake for 15 minutes.

4 Meanwhile, pour the reserved marinade into a small saucepan and bring to a boil over high heat. Cook until the liquid is reduced to a syrupy sauce, about 8 minutes.

5 Remove the drumettes from the oven and brush the tops with the reduced marinade. Flip the drumettes over, brush the other sides with the marinade, and continue to bake until the chicken is opaque throughout (no pink should show when you cut in next to a bone, and the chicken juices should run clear), about 10 minutes longer. Let cool slightly, sprinkle with the sesame seeds, then serve.

prep time: 10 minutes, plus 1 hour to marinate

cooking time: 25 minutes

½ cup maple syrup

¼ cup reduced-sodium soy sauce

1½ Tbsp peeled and grated fresh ginger

3 cloves garlic, minced

⅛ tsp pepper

2 lb chicken drumettes

Cooking spray

1–2 tsp sesame seeds, toasted

QUESO FUNDIDO

Serve this decadent dip with sturdy tortilla chips or soft corn tortillas for scooping up the crispy sausage and melted cheese. To make it vegetarian, substitute 1 cup coarsely chopped sautéed mushrooms for the chorizo. If you like it spicy, stir in ½ cup fire-roasted poblano chile strips with the tomato just before serving.

1 Preheat the oven to 350°F. In a frying pan, brown the chorizo over medium heat, stirring and breaking it up with a wooden spoon, until cooked through, about 6 minutes. Transfer the chorizo to a plate. Pour off all but about 1 Tbsp fat from the pan and add the onion. Cook, stirring occasionally, until soft, 6–7 minutes. Remove from the heat and stir in the cooked chorizo, tomato, and 1 Tbsp of the cilantro.

2 Spread half of the cheese across the bottom of a shallow baking dish. Top with the chorizo mixture and finish with the remaining cheese. Bake until the cheese melts, 4–5 minutes. Top with the remaining 1 Tbsp cilantro and serve with tortillas or chips for dipping.

prep time: 10 minutes
cooking time: 17 minutes

4 oz fresh Mexican chorizo, casing removed

½ yellow onion, chopped

1 Roma tomato, chopped

2 Tbsp chopped fresh cilantro

1 lb Monterey jack cheese, shredded

Small corn or flour tortillas or tortilla chips

HACK **REFRESH STALE TORTILLA CHIPS**

To restore the crispness to stale tortilla chips, spread them on a microwave-safe plate and microwave on high for 10–20 seconds just until warm. The chips will become crisp when cool.

POTATO SNACKS FOUR WAYS

Potatoes are a sure bet when it comes to versatility. Stuffed, dipped, wedged, or spiraled, potatoes are wonderfully accepting of a multitude of seasonings and uniformly bake up to boast a thin, crisp skin concealing a soft and tender interior.

Tornado Potato

1 Preheat the oven to 450°F. Soak a wooden skewer in water for 10 minutes. Push the soaked skewer lengthwise through the center of the potato. Holding a sharp knife at a slight diagonal and starting at one end, cut down to the skewer and continue cutting while turning the potato away from you to make spiraled rows about ½ inch apart. Separate the spiral so that air circulates between the rows.

2 Put the spiraled potato on a plate. Drizzle the butter evenly over the potato, turning and brushing with the butter to coat it evenly, then sprinkle all over with the seasonings.

3 Place the skewered potato in a baking dish so that the skewer ends rest on the rim of the dish and the potato is suspended. Bake until crisped on the outside and tender on the inside, about 50 minutes.

prep time: 10 minutes
cooking time: 50 minutes

---

1 russet potato, scrubbed and patted dry

2 Tbsp butter, melted

1 tsp seasoned salt or savory spice blend, such as Lawry's, shichimi togarashi, or Mrs. Dash

Sweet Potato Oven Fries with Sriracha Dip

1 Position a rack in the upper third of the oven and preheat to 450°F. Cut the potato lengthwise into ½-inch-thick slices, then cut the slices lengthwise into ½-inch-wide sticks. Pile the sticks on a rimmed baking sheet, drizzle with the oil, and toss to coat. Season with salt and pepper. Spread in an even layer on the baking sheet. Bake until golden and tender, about 50 minutes.

2 In a small bowl, mix the crème fraîche and Sriracha. Serve the fries hot from the oven with the dip alongside.

prep time: 10 minutes
cooking time: 50 minutes

---

1 sweet potato, peeled or scrubbed and patted dry

2 tsp olive oil

Salt and pepper

½ cup crème fraîche

1–2 tsp Sriracha

Potato Skins with Pancetta, Green Onions & Cheddar

1 Prick the potato all over with a fork, wrap in a paper towel, and place on a microwave-safe plate. Microwave on high until fork-tender, 3 minutes.

2 Meanwhile, in a frying pan, cook the pancetta, stirring often, until crispy, about 4 minutes.

3 Let the potato cool slightly, then cut in half lengthwise and remove most of the flesh, leaving ¼ inch around the perimeter. Reserve the potato flesh for another use.

4 Preheat the broiler. Place the baked potato skins, cut side down, on a baking sheet and brush both sides with the melted butter. Broil for 2 minutes, turn over, and continue to broil until the edges are golden brown, about 2 minutes longer.

5 Sprinkle the pancetta, green onions, and Cheddar into the potato skins, dividing them evenly. Return the filled skins to the broiler and broil just until the cheese is melted, about 2 minutes.

prep time: 2 minutes
cooking time: 10 minutes

---

1 sweet potato or russet potato, scrubbed and patted dry

10 oz diced pancetta or bacon

3 green onions, thinly sliced

2 cups shredded Cheddar cheese

1 Tbsp melted unsalted butter

Garlic-Parmesan Potato Wedges

1 Position a rack in the upper third of the oven and preheat to 450°F. Cut the potato lengthwise into wedges about 1 inch thick and pile them on a rimmed baking sheet. In a small microwave-safe bowl, combine the oil, butter, and garlic; microwave on high until the butter is melted, about 20 seconds.

2 Drizzle the garlic mixture over the wedges and toss to mix. Sprinkle with the Parmesan and season with salt and pepper; toss again to coat evenly, then spread out into a single layer. Bake until golden and tender when pierced with a knife, about 50 minutes.

prep time: 10 minutes
cooking time: 50 minutes

---

1 russet potato, scrubbed and patted dry

1 Tbsp olive oil

1 Tbsp unsalted butter

2 cloves garlic, minced

2 Tbsp grated Parmesan cheese

Salt and pepper

SOY-GLAZED EDAMAME

No fussy shelling required with these savory-sweet soy-glazed edamame pods. Simply insert a whole flavorful pod in your mouth and suck out the tender beans inside. Toss the edamame with the soy mixture while they're still warm from cooking to readily absorb the sauce.

1 Cook the edamame according to the package directions.

2 Meanwhile, warm the oil in a small frying pan over medium-low heat. Add the garlic and ginger and cook, stirring to prevent burning, until softened, 1–2 minutes. Stir in the soy sauce, water, vinegar, and brown sugar and cook, stirring, over medium heat until reduced slightly, about 1 minute.

3 When the edamame is ready, drain it in a colander set in the sink, then transfer it to a bowl. Pour the soy sauce mixture over the top and toss well to coat evenly. Sprinkle with the red pepper flakes and/or sesame seeds, and serve.

prep time: 5 minutes
cooking time: 10 minutes

1 package (12 oz) frozen edamame in the shell (about 4 cups)

1 tsp canola oil

1 small clove garlic, minced

1-inch piece fresh ginger, peeled and minced

2 Tbsp reduced-sodium soy sauce

2 Tbsp water

1 Tbsp rice vinegar

1½ Tbsp brown sugar

½ tsp red pepper flakes and/or toasted sesame seeds

HACK **PEEL FRESH GINGER**

To easily remove the skin from a knob of fresh ginger, rub it with the edge of a spoon.

MORE THAN JUST AVOCADO TOAST

Avocado toast makes for a tasty staple of the dorm room diet, but there can be a lot more to this easy snack than avocado. Start with a thick slice of good-quality bread (think artisanal and whole-grain), then get creative with toppings.

Squash, Ricotta & Pepitas

1 In a small frying pan, melt the butter over medium heat. Add the onion and cook, stirring constantly, until limp and lightly browned, about 4 minutes.

2 Spread each toast with 2 Tbsp of the ricotta, then add 2 Tbsp of the squash purée, spreading it evenly. Divide the onion equally among each toast, then top each one with 1 tsp of the pepitas and a sprinkling of chili powder.

prep time: 5 minutes

2 Tbsp unsalted butter

½ yellow onion, sliced

6 slices bread, toasted

¾ cup ricotta cheese

¾ cup Winter Squash Purée (page 123)

2 Tbsp roasted salted pepitas

Chili powder or za'atar seasoning for sprinkling

Eggplant, Feta & Pomegranate

1 Preheat the oven to 425°F. Spread the eggplant in a single layer on a rimmed baking sheet. Drizzle with the oil, toss to coat, and roast until browned and tender, 15–20 minutes. Let cool.

2 In a bowl, mix the eggplant with the feta, pomegranate seeds, parsley, and mint. Season to taste with salt and pepper. Stir in 1 tsp of the lemon juice, taste, and add more if needed. Divide the mixture evenly on the toasts.

prep time: 10 minutes
cooking time: 15 minutes

1 medium eggplant, cut into ½-inch dice

3 Tbsp olive oil

⅓ cup crumbled feta cheese

¼ cup pomegranate seeds

1 Tbsp chopped fresh parsley

1 tsp finely chopped fresh mint

Salt and pepper

1–2 tsp lemon juice

6 slices bread, toasted

Avocado, Cherry Tomatoes & Basil

1 Cut the avocado in half around the pit. Remove the pit, then cut slices into each avocado half without cutting through the skin.

2 Using a spoon, scoop out the slices from the skin and divide evenly among the toasts. Scatter an equal amount of the tomatoes over each toast, then sprinkle with the basil. Drizzle with olive oil and balsamic and season with salt and pepper.

prep time: 5 minutes

1 avocado

6 slices bread, toasted

½ pint cherry tomatoes, halved

6 Tbsp small fresh basil leaves

Olive oil and balsamic vinegar for drizzling

Salt and pepper

Mozzarella, Peach & Arugula

1 Cut the mozzarella into slices and divide equally among the toasts.

2 Scatter an equal amount of the peaches over each toast, then sprinkle with the arugula. Drizzle with olive oil.

prep time: 5 minutes

1 ball fresh mozzarella

6 slices bread, toasted

2 peaches, pitted and sliced

½ cup baby arugula leaves

Olive oil for drizzling

Dill Cream Cheese, Cucumber & Radish

1 Mix the cream cheese and dill in a small bowl.

2 Spread 2 Tbsp of the dill cream cheese over each toast, then add the cucumber and radishes, dividing them evenly. Top each toast with sprouts and season with salt and pepper.

prep time: 5 minutes

¾ cup cream cheese

1 tsp chopped fresh dill

6 slices bread, toasted

½ English cucumber, thinly sliced

6 radishes, thinly sliced

Alfalfa or other sprouts

Salt and pepper

Dill Cream
Cheese,
Cucumber
& Radish

EASY TOASTS

Make sure to have your favorite
ingredients on hand (prepared
in advance if needed), and
flavorful toasts like these will
come together quickly.

Eggplant,
Feta &
Pomegranate

Squash,
Ricotta
& Pepitas

Avocado,
Cherry
Tomatoes
& Basil

NO-BAKE ENERGY BITES

Loaded with nuts, oats, and dried fruits, these nutrition-packed bites are real food that will stave off hunger for hours. Enjoy them plain, or toss the sticky-sweet balls in a bowl of sweetened cocoa powder for a truffle-like finish, if you like.

1 Combine the apples, dates, vanilla, and zest in a food processor or blender and pulse until the mixture is well chopped and forms a ball, about 30 short pulses. Add the nuts, oats, pepitas, cinnamon, and salt and process until the nuts are finely ground

and the mixture forms moist clumps when pressed together with your fingers, about 2 minutes.

2 Roll the mixture between your palms into ¾-inch balls, placing them in a covered container. Serve right away, or cover and refrigerate for up to 1 month.

prep time: 10 minutes

¾ cup lightly packed chopped dried apples

½ cup pitted Medjool dates

1 tsp pure vanilla extract

1 tsp grated orange or lemon zest

1 cup lightly toasted nuts, such as walnuts or whole blanched almonds

¼ cup old-fashioned rolled oats

1 Tbsp pepitas or sesame seeds

1½ tsp ground cinnamon

¼ tsp salt

COOKING TIP

For the best flavor, spread the oats along with the nuts on a rimmed baking sheet and toast at 350°F until golden, about 8 minutes, before mixing them in.

SPICED CHICKPEAS

Chickpeas—also known as garbanzo beans—eclipse nuts, popcorn, and chips when it comes to nutrition. High in protein and fiber, wholesome chickpeas will fill you up and keep you sated for much longer than most other snack-time nibbles.

1 Preheat the oven to 400°F. Spread the chickpeas out on paper towels and pat dry, then transfer to a bowl. Add the oil and toss to coat evenly. Sprinkle on the cumin, chili powder, and salt and toss to mix evenly. Spread the chickpeas in an even layer on a rimmed baking sheet.

2 Bake until crispy and lightly browned, 30–40 minutes. Let cool, then serve. Store leftovers in a covered container at room temperature for up to 5 days.

prep time: 5 minutes
cooking time: 30 minutes

2 cans chickpeas (15 oz each), drained and rinsed

1 Tbsp olive oil

2 tsp ground cumin

2 tsp chili powder or smoked paprika

1 tsp salt

MICROWAVE IT

To make Spiced Chickpeas in the microwave, follow the directions above, mixing 1 can (15 oz) of chickpeas, 1 tsp olive oil, ½ tsp each ground cumin and chili powder, and ½ tsp salt in a microwave-safe bowl or plate. Cover loosely with a paper towel and microwave on high for 3 minutes. Stir well, cover with a paper towel, and microwave for 3 minutes longer. Remove from the microwave, remove the paper towel, and let stand until crispy, about 2 hours.

CHEESY OLIVE PULL-APART BREAD

All you need for this quick party snack is a loaf of good-quality bread, a trio of easy-to-source ingredients, and a hot oven. If you like, experiment with different ingredient combinations, such as Cheddar and jalapeño chile, Gorgonzola and crisp bacon, or fontina and cooked sausage.

1 Preheat the oven to 350°F. Using a long serrated knife, cut slits in the bread about 1 inch apart, being careful to not cut all the way through and leaving about ½ inch intact on the bottom. Rotate the bread and cut slits in the opposite direction, again 1 inch apart.

2 In a bowl, stir together the cheese, olives, and parsley. Using your hands, stuff the cheese mixture between the cuts, working in both directions. Place the loaf on a rimmed baking sheet and drizzle the butter all over the top.

3 Cover the loaf loosely with aluminum foil and bake for 15 minutes. Remove the foil and continue to bake until the cheese is melted and the top of the bread is golden brown, about 10 minutes longer. Transfer to a platter and serve.

prep time: 20 minutes
cooking time: 25 minutes

---

1 round loaf artisanal bread

2 cups shredded Gruyère cheese

⅔ cup pitted Kalamata olives, coarsely chopped

⅓ cup loosely packed fresh parsley leaves, chopped

4 Tbsp (½ stick) unsalted butter, melted

HACK **STAVE OFF MOLDY CHEESE**

To help prevent cheese from becoming moldy, dampen a paper towel with vinegar and place it and the cheese in a covered container or lock-top plastic bag in the refrigerator during storage.

DINNER

MAKES 3 SERVINGS

ROASTED VEGETABLE BUDDHA BOWL WITH SALSA VERDE

The theory behind a Buddha bowl is that you slow down long enough to mindfully appreciate each ingredient. Roast all the vegetables in the same pan, then arrange them beautifully in your bowl. For a shortcut, skip the salsa verde and add minced parsley and cilantro to your favorite vinaigrette instead.

1 Preheat the oven to 425°F. Pour 1 Tbsp of the oil into a bowl. Season with salt and pepper.

2 Working with one vegetable at a time and starting with the lightest in color, peel and then cut the vegetable into ¾-inch dice. Transfer the diced vegetable to the bowl, toss to coat, then arrange in a single layer on a rimmed baking sheet. Repeat to peel, cut, and coat the remaining root vegetables, adding as little additional oil as possible to coat the vegetables and arranging

them side by side on the baking sheet (but keeping them separate). Repeat with the green beans or asparagus. Roast the vegetables until lightly browned and tender, about 15 minutes for green beans and asparagus and 20 minutes for sweet potato, carrot, and beet.

3 Meanwhile, prepare the salsa verde and set aside.

4 Stir the nuts into the farro, then spoon into bowls. Arrange the roasted vegetables in rows on top, drizzle with salsa verde, and serve.

prep time: 10 minutes
cooking time: 20 minutes

4–6 Tbsp olive oil

Salt and pepper

1½ lb assorted root vegetables, such as sweet potato, carrot, and/or beet

4 oz green beans or asparagus

Salsa Verde (page 124)

¼ cup lightly toasted finely chopped pecans, hazelnuts, walnuts, or pine nuts

3 cups cooked Farro, Rice, or Quinoa (page 122)

CHICKEN, BROCCOLI & CASHEW STIR-FRY

For a meal that comes together in minutes, have all the ingredients prepped and ready to go and make sure your pan is very hot before you start cooking. To check the heat of your pan, toss a drop of water into it; if it sizzles, the pan is ready.

1 In a large bowl, whisk together 1½ tsp of the soy sauce, the vinegar, and ¼ tsp of the cornstarch. Season with salt and pepper and add the chicken. Toss the chicken in the marinade and let stand at room temperature for 10 minutes.

2 In a small bowl, whisk together the broth, oyster sauce, remaining 1½ tsp soy sauce, and remaining ¼ tsp cornstarch. Set aside.

3 Meanwhile, bring a saucepan of salted water to a boil over high heat. Add the broccoli and cook until tender-crisp, about 3 minutes. Drain well and set aside.

4 Warm a wok or a large nonstick frying pan over high heat. When the pan is very hot, add the chicken and all of its marinade and toss and stir until the chicken is opaque throughout, about 6 minutes. Stir in the ginger and garlic and cook just until fragrant, about 30 seconds. Stir in the oyster sauce mixture and let simmer, stirring once or twice, until the sauce thickens, about 2 minutes. Stir in the cashews and broccoli.

5 Serve the stir-fry alongside the rice. Pass the hot sauce at the table, if using. To store leftovers, let cool, then store in an airtight container in the refrigerator for up to 4 days.

prep time: 15 minutes
cooking time: 15 minutes

---

1 Tbsp low-sodium soy sauce

1 tsp rice vinegar

½ tsp cornstarch

Salt and pepper

½ lb boneless, skinless chicken breasts, cut into ½-inch cubes

2 Tbsp reduced-sodium chicken broth or water

1 Tbsp oyster sauce

⅓ lb broccoli, trimmed and cut into small florets

1 Tbsp peeled and minced fresh ginger

1 clove garlic, minced

2 Tbsp cashews

Steamed Rice (page 122) for serving

Hot pepper sauce for serving (optional)

GINGER-SOY GLAZED CHICKEN THIGHS

The sweet soy marinade for this budget-friendly chicken cut doubles as a flavorful glaze after it is boiled down on the stovetop—a step that also removes any of the natural bacteria it may have picked up from the chicken.

1 In a shallow nonaluminum dish, combine the sugar, soy sauce, ginger, garlic, and 1 tsp of the oil. Stir until blended and the sugar dissolves. Add the chicken thighs and stir to coat. Cover and let marinate in the refrigerator for at least 30 minutes or up to 1 day.

2 In a frying pan, warm the remaining 1 tsp oil over medium heat. Remove the chicken thighs from the marinade, reserving the marinade, and add them to the pan. Cook, turning once, until browned and cooked through, 10–12 minutes total; watch carefully and turn down the heat if the glaze starts to burn. Transfer the thighs to a plate.

3 Pour the reserved marinade into the frying pan and boil until reduced to a glaze, about 1 minute; do not burn. Remove the pan from the heat, add the chicken thighs, and turn to coat with the glaze. Serve.

prep time: 5 minutes, plus 30 minutes to marinate
cooking time: 10 minutes

¼ cup golden brown sugar

3 Tbsp reduced-sodium soy sauce

1 Tbsp peeled and minced fresh ginger

2 cloves garlic, minced

2 tsp canola oil

4 boneless, skinless chicken thighs (about 1¼ lb)

HACK **PEEL A GARLIC CLOVE WITH EASE**

To remove the papery sheath from a clove of garlic, put the clove on a work surface, lay the side of a chef's knife over the clove, and whack the knife with the palm of your hand. The sheath will break and slip off easily.

SAUTÉED CHICKEN BREASTS WITH WARM TOMATO SALAD

Pounding chicken breasts both tenderizes the meat and cuts cooking time. A hot pan quickly sautés the chicken, then warms the tomatoes in their juices. Use the best cherry tomatoes you can find, preferably in an assortment of colors.

1 Put the chicken breasts on a cutting board. With the knife parallel to the cutting board, cut each breast into 2 thin halves. One at a time, place each piece of the breast meat between 2 pieces of plastic wrap and lightly pound with a meat pounder or smooth rock to a thickness of ¼-½ inch. Season the chicken generously on both sides with salt and pepper.

2 In a large nonstick frying pan, warm the olive oil over medium-high heat. Add the chicken and reduce the heat to medium. Cook, turning once, until nicely browned and opaque throughout, 3–4 minutes per side. Transfer the cooked pieces to a platter and cover with aluminum foil to keep warm.

3 Add the shallot and garlic to the pan and cook, stirring often, until softened, 3–4 minutes. Add the tomatoes and vinegar and cook, stirring often, until the tomatoes begin to soften and split, about 4 minutes. Stir in the basil and season with salt and pepper.

4 For each serving, place a chicken breast on a plate and spoon some of the tomato mixture on top. To store leftovers, let cool, then transfer to an airtight container and refrigerate for up to 3 days. Reheat before serving.

prep time: 15 minutes
cooking time: 15 minutes

---

2 boneless, skinless chicken breast halves, about 6 oz each

Salt and pepper

1 Tbsp olive oil

1 large shallot, minced

1 small clove garlic, minced

½ pint (about 1 cup) cherry and/or pear tomatoes, preferably a mix of colors and shapes, halved

1½ Tbsp balsamic vinegar

¼ cup packed fresh basil leaves, torn

HOLIDAY-WORTHY ROAST TURKEY BREAST

Roasting a turkey breast beats roasting the whole bird. The breast is easy to turn, allowing it to self-baste as it roasts. For a stress-free holiday meal, serve the turkey with Mashed Potatoes (page 122) and Microwave Cranberry Sauce (page 125).

1 Position a rack in the lower third of the oven and preheat to 450°F. Place the 2 onion halves in the center of a roasting pan. Line up the carrots and celery on either side. If using the garlic, tuck it in among the other vegetables.

2 Rinse the turkey breast and pat dry with paper towels. Season all over with salt and pepper. Set the breast, skin side down, on top of the vegetables. Pour in 3 cups of the broth.

3 Roast the turkey for 30 minutes. Reduce the oven temperature to 325°F. Turn the breast to rest on one side and baste with the liquid in the pan. Roast for another 30 minutes. Turn the breast to rest on the opposite side, and baste again with the pan liquid. Roast

for another 30 minutes. Turn the breast skin-side-up in the pan and baste again. If the liquid has begun to evaporate, add the remaining 1 cup broth to the pan. Roast for 30 minutes, baste, and then continue roasting until an instant-read thermometer inserted into the thickest part away from the bone registers 165°F, 2–2½ hours total (figure on 20 minutes per pound). If the top of the breast begins to overbrown, tent loosely with aluminum foil.

4 Remove the turkey from the oven and transfer to a cutting board. Let rest for 20 minutes. Carve into slices and serve right away. Store leftovers in a covered container in the refrigerator for up to 5 days.

prep time: 10 minutes
cooking time: 2 hours

---

1 large yellow onion, halved

2 large carrots

2 large ribs celery

1 clove garlic, peeled (optional)

1 bone-in whole turkey breast, 6–8 lb

Salt and pepper

3–4 cups reduced-sodium chicken broth

YELLOW CHICKEN CURRY WITH POTATOES & CARROTS

Make this classic Thai curry on Sunday to have enough leftovers for the rest of the week. For a shortcut, substitute cut-up rotisserie chicken for the chicken pieces; skip the searing step and add the cooked chicken during the last 10 minutes of cooking.

1 Preheat the oven to 325°F. Sprinkle the chicken pieces evenly with 1 tsp of the salt. Warm a Dutch oven or large oven-safe frying pan over high heat until very hot and add the oil. Add the chicken, skin side down, and sear until browned and crisp, 5–6 minutes. Turn the pieces and sear again, 5–6 minutes longer. Using tongs or a slotted spoon, transfer the chicken to a plate.

2 Add the onion, ginger, and garlic to the pot and cook, stirring, until just tender, about 2 minutes. Stir in the curry powder and cook for 10 seconds longer. Add the coconut milk, water, lemon juice, and remaining 1 tsp salt and bring to a boil. Return the chicken pieces to the pan and simmer for 2 minutes.

3 Cover the pan tightly, transfer to the oven, and bake for 30 minutes. Remove from the oven, stir in the potatoes and carrots, cover, and return to the oven. Continue to bake until the potatoes and carrots are tender, about 30 minutes longer. Uncover and cook for a final 10 minutes to allow the curry to thicken. Serve with the rice. To store leftovers, let cool, then transfer to an airtight container and refrigerate for up to 4 days. Reheat before serving.

prep time: 15 minutes
cooking time: 1½ hours

---

2 lb bone-in, skin-on chicken breasts and/or thighs

2 tsp salt

2 Tbsp vegetable or peanut oil

1 yellow onion, chopped

1 Tbsp peeled and minced fresh ginger

3 cloves garlic, minced

1½ Tbsp curry powder

1 can (13.5 oz) unsweetened coconut milk

½ cup water

Juice of 1 lemon

2 large boiling potatoes, peeled and cut into large cubes

2 carrots, peeled and cut into large pieces

Steamed Rice (page 122) for serving

BEER-BAKED PULLED PORK

A nonalcoholic brew is fine for this tender slow-cooked pork. Cook the meat on Sunday and you'll have more than enough to last for the rest of the week. Try it in tacos, sandwiches, bowls, or quesadillas (recipes follow).

1 Preheat the oven to 250°F. In a large Dutch oven or heavy-bottomed pot, heat the oil over high heat. Sprinkle the pork butt generously all over with salt and pepper. Add the pork to the pot and sear, turning as needed, until a slight crust forms on all sides, about 15 minutes total.

2 Pour the beer over the pork butt. Add the onion, sugar, and chili powder to the pot and mix well. Cover the pot and roast for 6 hours.

3 Remove the pot from the oven and use 2 forks to test the pork; it should shred easily. If it doesn't, cover and continue roasting until it comes apart with no resistance, up to 1 hour longer. Remove from the oven and let rest for 10 minutes, then transfer the pork butt to a cutting board or platter and shred it with your fingers, discarding any big pieces of fat. Return the meat to the pot and stir it into the juices, then return the pot to the oven and allow the pork to simmer in the juices for another 1–2 hours, or until serving time.

prep time: 5 minutes
cooking time: 8 hours

2 Tbsp vegetable oil
4 lb pork butt
Salt and pepper
1 can (12 fl oz) beer
1 large yellow onion, chopped
¼ cup firmly packed golden brown sugar
1 Tbsp chili powder

Continued on page 84

Continued from page 83

VARIATIONS

Pork Soft Taco with Pineapple Salsa & Red Cabbage Slaw

Place a frying pan over medium heat. When the pan is hot, add 2 taco-size flour tortillas and heat, turning once, until puffy and lightly browned on both sides, about 3 minutes total. Spoon 2 Tbsp pulled pork into each tortilla, then top each one with 1 Tbsp each pineapple salsa (page 124) and shredded red cabbage. Serve with lime wedges.

Pulled Pork Sandwich

Mix ½ cup warm pulled pork with 2–3 Tbsp store-bought barbecue sauce. Pile the pork mixture onto the bottom of a sandwich bun, top with about ¼ cup store-bought coleslaw, then add the bun top.

Bánh Mì Bowl

Spoon 1 cup hot, steamed jasmine rice (page 122) into a serving bowl. Top with ½ cup warm pulled pork; ¼ cucumber, sliced; 1 radish, thinly sliced; pickled carrots; and 1 jalapeño chile, sliced, arranging all the ingredients attractively. Garnish with fresh cilantro leaves.

Pork & Cheddar Quesadilla

Cut ⅓ yellow onion into slices. Warm 2 tsp olive oil in a frying pan over medium-high heat. Add the onion and sauté quickly, stirring often, until browned and tender, 3–4 minutes. Transfer the onion to a plate and set aside. Return the pan to medium heat. Place 1 flour tortilla in the pan and add ½ cup shredded Cheddar cheese, ½ cup pulled pork, 2 Tbsp roasted red pepper, and the reserved sautéed onion, spreading it evenly. Top with another tortilla and cook, turning once, until lightly browned and the cheese is melted, 2–3 minutes.

Pork, Mango & Avocado Summer Rolls

Cut ¼ mango and ¼ avocado into thin slices. Set aside, along with ⅓ cup pulled pork, 2 butter lettuce leaves, a small handful of bean sprouts, and 1 Tbsp each cilantro and mint leaves. Fill a wide, shallow bowl with hot water. Slip one 8½-inch rice paper round into the hot water, submerge it for a few seconds, then lay it flat on the work surface. Line up horizontal rows of half each of the lettuce, mango, avocado, pork, sprouts, and herbs along the bottom third of the softened rice paper. Fold the bottom edge of the wrapper up and over the filling. Fold the open right side over the filling, then the left. Pressing the wrapper tightly over the filling, roll it away from you into a snug cylinder. Repeat with another rice paper round and the remaining filling ingredients. Serve with Chile Dipping Sauce (page 125).

STIR-FRIED PORK & SUGAR SNAPS WITH SOBA NOODLES

If you enjoy a good stir-fry, you'll likely have these pantry ingredients at the ready. Soba noodles are a nice addition, but feel free to use spaghetti instead. Double the recipe if you want to serve more.

1 In a bowl, combine 1½ Tbsp of the soy sauce and the cornstarch and stir to dissolve the cornstarch. Mix in 1½ tsp of the sesame oil. Add the pork and a generous amount of black pepper and stir to coat. Let marinate for 15–30 minutes.

2 Meanwhile, in a small cup, combine the remaining 2 Tbsp soy sauce, remaining 1 Tbsp sesame oil, the vinegar, and sugar and stir to dissolve the sugar. Set aside.

3 Fill a large pot three-quarters full of water and bring to a boil over high heat. Add the sugar snap peas and cook until just tender-crisp, about 4 minutes. Using a slotted spoon, transfer the peas to a bowl. Add the noodles to the boiling water and cook, stirring occasionally, until just tender, about 4 minutes. Drain the noodles, then return them to the empty pot. Add half of the sauce to the noodles and stir to coat. Mix in the sugar snaps and all but 2 Tbsp of the green onions. Cover to keep warm.

4 In a large nonstick frying pan, warm the peanut oil over medium-high heat. Add the ginger and red pepper flakes and stir until fragrant, about 5 seconds. Add the pork (reserving the marinade) and cook, stirring constantly and separating the pieces, just until the pork is cooked through, 2–3 minutes. Add the remaining marinade and stir until the sauce thickens, about 30 seconds. Immediately add the pork and sauce to the noodles, then toss to coat. Sprinkle with the reserved green onions and serve. To store leftovers, let cool, then store in an airtight container in the refrigerator for up to 4 days.

prep time: 30 minutes
cooking time: 15 minutes

3½ Tbsp reduced-sodium soy sauce

1½ tsp cornstarch

1½ Tbsp toasted sesame oil

½ lb boneless pork sirloin, cut across the grain into thin strips

Ground black pepper to taste

2 Tbsp rice vinegar

1½ tsp sugar

½ lb sugar snap peas, cut in half on the diagonal

6 oz soba noodles

1 bunch green onions, white and green parts thinly sliced

1 Tbsp peanut or vegetable oil

1 Tbsp peeled and minced fresh ginger

¼ tsp red pepper flakes

PIZZA WITH TOPPINGS GALORE

For the best results with store-bought pizza dough, bring it to room temperature and don't overwork it while shaping; place the baking sheet with the pizza on the lowest oven rack; and preheat your oven to the hottest temperature on your dial.

1 Position an oven rack in the lowest part of the oven and preheat to 450°F for at least 15 minutes. Sprinkle a rimless baking sheet with coarsely ground cornmeal.

2 Press and stretch the pizza dough into a 15-inch round and place on the baking sheet. Top with the desired sauce and toppings below. Bake until the crust is golden brown, 10–12 minutes. Cut into wedges and serve.

prep time: 10 minutes
cooking time: 15 minutes

Coarse cornmeal for dusting
1 ball store-bought pizza dough
Toppings (see below)

VARIATIONS

Kale + Pancetta + Lemon
In a small bowl, mix 1 cup White Pizza Sauce (page 125), ½ tsp grated lemon zest, and 2 tsp lemon juice and spread over the round of pizza dough. (Alternatively, pull 8 oz burrata into pieces, drop evenly over the dough, and sprinkle the zest and juice on top.) Scatter ¼ cup shredded mozzarella cheese over the sauce, then sprinkle with ½ cup baby kale leaves that have been lightly tossed with olive oil, ¼ cup cooked sliced pancetta or bacon, and another ¼ cup shredded mozzarella. Bake as directed.

Sausage + Fennel + Black Olive
Spread ⅓ cup store-bought pizza sauce evenly over the round of pizza dough. Sprinkle with ½ cup cooked sausage meat, ¾ cup shredded mozzarella cheese, ¼ bulb very thinly sliced fennel, and 2 cloves thinly sliced garlic. Drizzle with 1 Tbsp olive oil. Bake as directed.

Mushroom + Fontina + Sun-Dried Tomato
In a frying pan over medium-high heat, sauté 5 oz sliced mushrooms in 2 Tbsp olive oil until lightly browned, about 5 minutes. Add 2 cloves minced garlic and cook, stirring, for 1 minute. Spread 1 cup store-bought pizza sauce evenly over the round of pizza dough. Sprinkle with 1½ cups shredded fontina cheese, the cooked mushrooms, and 2 Tbsp chopped sun-dried tomatoes. Bake as directed.

SHORTCUT SPAGHETTI BOLOGNESE

This recipe makes plenty of Bolognese. Freeze half for eating later: Spoon the sauce by the cupful into lock-top sandwich bags for individual servings, then freeze for up to 3 months. Thaw each bag separately when you're ready to eat. Serve it over pasta (as here), or try it atop soft-cooked polenta or a thick slice of pan-fried eggplant.

1 In a large frying pan, warm the oil over medium-low heat. Add the ground beef, onion, and garlic and cook, stirring to break up the meat, until the meat is no longer pink, 5–7 minutes. Pour off any fat. Return the pan to the heat and stir in the marinara, oregano, and basil (if using). Bring to a boil over medium heat, then reduce the heat to medium-low, cover partially, and simmer until thickened slightly, about 20 minutes. Remove from the heat and cover to keep warm. (If making the sauce ahead, remove it from the heat and let cool, then cover and refrigerate for up to 4 days, or transfer to a heavy-duty lock-top plastic bag and freeze for up to 3 months.)

2 Bring a large pot of salted water to a boil. Add the pasta, stir, and cook according to the package directions. Using a glass measuring cup, scoop out about ½ cup of the cooking water and set aside. Drain the pasta, then add it to the Bolognese and toss quickly until well blended and hot, adding a little of the reserved pasta cooking water if needed to loosen the sauce. Serve, passing the Parmesan at the table.

prep time: 5 minutes
cooking time: 35 minutes

---

2 Tbsp olive oil

1 lb ground beef

1 yellow onion, finely chopped

4 cloves garlic, minced

1 jar (24 oz) store-bought marinara sauce

2 Tbsp dried oregano

2 tsp dried basil (optional)

1½ lb dried pasta or 2 lb fresh pasta

Grated Parmesan cheese for serving

THE ULTIMATE MAC & CHEESE

This is the dish to make when you feel like real comfort food. It makes enough to share, or to eat for the rest of the week. To reheat the leftovers, drizzle with a splash of milk, cover with aluminum foil, and slip into a 350°F oven until heated through.

1 Preheat the oven to 350°F. Butter a shallow 3-qt baking dish.

2 In a large frying pan, melt 3 Tbsp of the butter over medium-low heat. Add the garlic and cook, stirring frequently, until tender but not browned, about 3 minutes. Add the bread crumbs and stir until coated with butter. Remove from the heat and set aside.

3 Bring a large pot of salted water to a boil over high heat. Add the pasta, stir, and cook according to the package directions until not quite al dente. (The macaroni will continue to cook in the oven, so do not cook it fully now.) Drain well and set aside.

4 Put the pot used for the pasta over medium heat and melt the remaining 4 Tbsp butter. Whisk in the flour. Reduce the heat to medium-low and cook, stirring, for 1 minute. Gradually whisk in the milk, raise the heat to medium, and bring to a boil, whisking frequently. Remove from the heat and stir in the cheeses and mustard. Season with salt and pepper. Stir in the pasta. Spread in the prepared baking dish and sprinkle evenly with the buttered bread crumbs.

5 Bake until the bread crumbs are browned and the sauce is bubbling, about 20 minutes. Let cool for 5 minutes, then serve.

prep time: 5 minutes
cooking time: 35 minutes

---

7 Tbsp unsalted butter, plus more for greasing

1 clove garlic, minced

1½ cups coarse fresh bread crumbs

Salt and pepper

1 lb elbow macaroni

¼ cup all-purpose flour

3 cups whole milk, warmed

2 cups shredded sharp Cheddar cheese

2 cups shredded fontina cheese

½ tsp dry mustard

COOKING TIP

Any tubular pasta works well in this recipe. Some favorites are penne, ziti, or mostaccioli. You can also try adding chopped crisp bacon, cubes of smoked ham or cooked chicken, cooked peas, chopped blanched broccoli, cooked wild mushrooms, or crumbled blue cheese when you stir in the cheese.

PENNE WITH CAULIFLOWER PESTO

Charring cauliflower brings out its naturally nutty flavor. Paired with almonds and Parmesan, the versatile veggie makes a tasty pesto that saves well. Refrigerate leftovers in a covered container for up to 4 days and reheat before serving.

1 Preheat a stovetop grill pan or frying pan over high heat.

2 Season the cauliflower florets with salt and pepper. Place in the hot pan and cook, turning occasionally, until well charred on all sides, 6–8 minutes. Transfer to a food processor or blender and add the oil, parsley, almonds, capers, and garlic. Pulse until the mixture is well combined but still coarse. Set aside.

3 Bring a large pot of salted water to a boil. Add the pasta, stir, and cook according to the package directions until al dente. Drain and transfer to a serving bowl. Add the cauliflower pesto and Parmesan and toss to combine, then serve.

prep time: 10 minutes
cooking time: 15 minutes

---

1 small head cauliflower,
cored and cut into 1-inch florets

Salt and pepper

1 cup olive oil

1 cup lightly packed fresh
parsley leaves

½ cup toasted almonds

2 Tbsp capers

2 cloves garlic, minced

1 lb penne

½ cup grated Parmesan cheese

SKILLET SAUSAGE & BEEF LASAGNA

One sturdy skillet is all that's required to bake up this hearty lasagna. Even if you share some with friends, you will likely still have enough left over to cover several meals. No-boil lasagna noodles are a good time-saving alternative to dried.

1 Preheat the oven to 375°F. In a 12-inch cast-iron skillet or other oven-safe frying pan, warm the oil over medium-high heat. Add the ground beef and cook, stirring occasionally, until browned, 4–6 minutes. Transfer to a plate. Pour off all but 1 Tbsp fat from the skillet.

2 Return the skillet to medium-high heat, add the onion and garlic, and cook, stirring occasionally, until the onion is translucent, 4–6 minutes. Add the oregano and red pepper flakes and cook, stirring occasionally, for 30 seconds. Return the ground beef to the skillet, stir in the crushed tomatoes, and season with salt and black pepper. Transfer the sauce to a large bowl and reserve the skillet.

3 In a medium bowl, stir together the ricotta, 1 cup of the mozzarella, ¼ cup of the Parmesan, the basil, egg, and a large pinch each of salt and black pepper.

4 Spread ⅓ cup of the sauce evenly over the bottom of the skillet. Cover with a single layer of 3 lasagna noodles (break up the noodles into smaller pieces to fill in any gaps). Top with ⅓ cup of the ricotta mixture, then ⅓ cup of the sauce, ¾ cup of the mozzarella, ¼ cup of the Parmesan, and another layer of 3 lasagna noodles. Repeat the layering of sauce, noodles, ricotta mixture, and cheeses three more times. Cover with the remaining 3 lasagna noodles, then top with the remaining sauce, mozzarella, and Parmesan.

5 Cover the skillet loosely with aluminum foil and bake for 20 minutes. Remove the foil and continue to bake until the lasagna is browned and bubbly, about 25 minutes longer. Let rest for 15 minutes, then serve. To store any leftovers, let cool, then store in a covered container in the refrigerator for up to 4 days.

prep time: 15 minutes
cooking time: 45 minutes

2 Tbsp olive oil

1 lb ground beef, or a mix of bulk pork sausage and ground beef

1 yellow onion, diced

3 cloves garlic, minced

2 tsp dried oregano

Pinch red pepper flakes

1 big can (28 oz) plus 1 little can (14 oz) crushed tomatoes

Salt and ground black pepper

1 container (15 oz) ricotta cheese

4½ cups shredded mozzarella cheese

1½ cups grated Parmesan cheese

1 cup packed fresh basil leaves, roughly chopped

1 large egg, lightly beaten

15 no-boil lasagna noodles

CLASSIC HERB-ROASTED CHICKEN

Not much is needed to roast a whole chicken to near perfection. A dash of salt and pepper, some garlic, a fresh herb sprig, and an hour in a hot oven results in tender, well-seasoned meat that is tasty on its own or added to a range of dishes.

1 Preheat the oven to 425°F. Remove the giblets from the chicken and discard (or reserve for another use). Rinse the chicken inside and out and pat dry with paper towels. Generously season the chicken inside and out with salt and pepper. Shove the herbs and garlic (if using) inside the chicken cavity. Bring the wing tips up toward the neck and tuck them around to the back of the chicken. Using kitchen twine, tie the chicken legs together at the ankles. Place the chicken in a roasting pan and rub all over with the oil or butter.

2 Roast the chicken, basting once or twice with the pan juices during baking, until an instant-read thermometer inserted into the thickest part of a thigh but away from the bone registers 165°F, or until the juices run clear when cut with a knife, about 1¼ hours. To store any leftover chicken, let cool, transfer to a heavy-duty lock-top plastic bag, and refrigerate for up to 4 days.

prep time: 5 minutes
cooking time: 1 hour 15 minutes

1 roasting chicken, 5–6 lb
Salt and pepper
1–2 sprigs fresh thyme or rosemary (optional)
2 garlic cloves, crushed (optional)
1 Tbsp olive oil or room temperature butter

VARIATIONS

Chicken-Tortilla Soup (page 41)
Chinese Chicken Salad (page 44)
Chicken Caesar Salad (page 45)
Greek-Style Salad with Chicken (page 51)

BLOODY MARY TRI-TIP

Bottled Bloody Mary mix has all the necessary ingredients of a good marinade: zesty vegetable juice, Worcestershire sauce, celery salt, horseradish, and plenty of seasonings. Enjoy the tri-tip as is, or slice it to beef up soups and salads.

1 In a large heavy-duty lock-top plastic bag, combine the Bloody Mary mix with the lime juice. Add the meat, seal closed, and massage the meat to coat. Let marinate in the refrigerator for 2–12 hours. Before cooking, bring the meat to room temperature in the marinade, then wipe the marinade from the meat, pat dry with paper towels, and season with salt and pepper.

2 **TO ROAST THE TRI-TIP,** preheat the oven to 450°F. Coat a roasting pan with cooking spray. Place the meat, fat side up, in the roasting pan and roast for 15 minutes. Reduce the oven temperature to 350°F and continue roasting until an instant-read thermometer inserted into the meat reads 140°F for medium-rare, 20–25 minutes longer.

3 **TO GRILL THE TRI-TIP,** prepare a charcoal or gas grill for indirect heat cooking. If using a charcoal grill, bank the coals on either side of the center. If using a gas grill, turn off one burner and preheat the rest. Lightly coat the grill rack with cooking spray. Place the meat on the grill rack directly over the heat and sear, turning as needed, until browned, about 10 minutes. Move the meat to the cooler side of the grill and continue to cook, turning as needed to prevent burning, until evenly browned on the outside and an instant-read thermometer inserted into the meat reads 140°F for medium-rare, 12–15 minutes longer.

prep time: 5 minutes, plus at least 2 hours to marinate

cooking time: 35 minutes to roast or 15 minutes to grill

---

1 cup bottled Bloody Mary mix

Juice from ½ lime

1 beef tri-tip roast (about 1½ lb)

Salt and pepper

Cooking spray

VARIATIONS

Greek-Style Beef Salad (page 51)

STIR-FRIED BEEF & BOK CHOY

Flank steak is a good choice, but you can use any cut of beef for this 15-minute dish. Bok choy has wonderful crisp texture and flavor similar to celery. It's best cooked until tender but still crisp. Serve this dish atop rice noodles or steamed brown rice.

1 In a small bowl, stir together the sherry, soy sauce, and chile paste. Cut the bok choy lengthwise into halves or quarters, depending on size.

2 In a wok or large frying pan, heat 1½ tsp of the oil over high heat. Add the bok choy and stir-fry just until tender-crisp, 3–4 minutes. Transfer to a bowl.

3 Add the remaining ½ tsp oil to the pan. Add the garlic and ginger and stir-fry until fragrant but not browned, 15–30 seconds. Add the beef and cook, stirring, just until no longer pink, about 2 minutes.

4 Return the bok choy to the pan, add the sherry mixture, and cook for 1 minute, or until heated through. Serve.

prep time: 5 minutes
cooking time: 10 minutes

---

2 Tbsp dry sherry
or orange juice

1 Tbsp soy sauce

½ tsp Asian chile paste
or Sriracha

1 lb baby bok choy

2 tsp peanut oil

2 cloves garlic, minced

1 Tbsp peeled and grated
fresh ginger

1 lb flank steak, thinly
sliced across the grain

HACK **SLICE MEAT PAPER-THIN**

To cut large pieces of meat into super-thin restaurant-worthy slices, freeze the meat for 30 minutes before slicing it with a sharp knife.

PARTY-SIZE CHILI CON CARNE

When game night is at your place, this is the dish to put on the table. Cook up a big pot and set it out with a range of toppings for guests to add, such as sliced chiles, chopped onion, corn kernels, sour cream, and corn chips.

1 In a large heavy pot, warm the oil over medium heat. Add the onion and cook, stirring often, until translucent, about 5 minutes. Add the ground beef and garlic and cook, using a wooden spoon to break up the meat into small pieces, until the beef is browned, 5–7 minutes. Pour off the fat from the pan.

2 Add the chili powder, cumin, basil, and oregano and stir to mix well. Stir in the chicken broth, crushed tomatoes, and tomato paste. Reduce the heat to medium-low and simmer, stirring occasionally, until the mixture has a thick, chunky consistency, about 1 hour. (At this point, you can let cool, cover, and refrigerate for up to 3 days. Reheat before continuing.)

3 Five minutes before serving, stir in the beans and simmer until heated through. Season with salt and pepper. Spoon the chili into individual bowls, sprinkle the cheese evenly over the tops, and serve.

prep time: 10 minutes
cooking time: 1 hour 15 minutes

---

2 Tbsp olive oil

1 yellow onion, chopped

3 lb ground beef

8 cloves garlic, minced

⅓ cup chili powder

1 Tbsp ground cumin

1 tsp dried basil

1 tsp dried oregano

4 cups reduced-sodium chicken broth

1 can (28 oz) crushed tomatoes

½ cup tomato paste

2 cans (15½ oz each) chili beans in sauce

Salt and pepper

1 cup shredded Cheddar cheese

SERVING TIP

There are many outside-of-the-bowl options for serving chili. Try spooning it into a small, round hollowed-out bread loaf, or over nachos (page 56), a bowl of corn chips, or your favorite hot dog.

ONE-PAN SOY-GLAZED SALMON

You can't go wrong with a good soy-based marinade for salmon. A touch of brown sugar creates a sweet glaze that nicely cloaks the fillet. It cooks well on a grill pan or nonstick frying pan, or try it on an outdoor grill if you have access to one.

1 In a large heavy-duty lock-top plastic bag, mix the mustard, soy sauce, sugar, and garlic. Add the fillet and massage to coat. Cover and refrigerate for at least 45 minutes. Remove from the refrigerator 15 minutes before cooking.

2 Place a grill pan or nonstick frying pan over medium-high heat. When the pan is hot, place the fillet, skin side down, in the pan. Cook, turning once, until caramelized on both sides but still rosy pink and moist in the center, 4–6 minutes total. Serve hot.

prep time: 5 minutes
cooking time: 5 minutes

---

1 Tbsp Dijon mustard

1 Tbsp soy sauce

1½ tsp firmly packed dark brown sugar

1 small clove garlic, minced

1 skin-on salmon fillet, about ¼ lb and 1 inch thick, pin bones removed

FOIL-PACKET COD WITH TOMATOES, OLIVES & SPINACH

Cooking fish inside a foil packet traps flavors and aromas inside, making this recipe a good one to prepare if you would like to keep the scent of your freshly cooked fillet to yourself. Even better, this method is completely hands-off. Wrap all the ingredients in a piece of foil, seal, and bake. In 15 minutes, your meal is ready.

1 Preheat the oven to 375°F. Place a 12-inch piece of aluminum foil on a rimmed baking sheet.

2 Scatter the spinach over half of the foil. Drizzle 1½ tsp of the oil over the spinach and season with salt and pepper. Place the cod fillet on the spinach and top with the tomatoes, olives, and rosemary. Drizzle with the remaining 1½ tsp oil, season generously with salt and pepper, and squeeze the lemon wedge over the top.

3 Fold the uncovered half of the foil over the fish and crimp the edges to seal the fish inside. Bake until the fish is opaque throughout, about 15 minutes. Transfer the fish and vegetables from the foil packet to a plate and serve.

prep time: 3 minutes
cooking time: 15 minutes

1 cup packed baby spinach

1 Tbsp olive oil

Salt and pepper

1 cod fillet (about 6 oz)

5 cherry tomatoes, halved

2 Tbsp cured black olives, pitted and halved

½ tsp dried rosemary

1 lemon wedge

DESSERTS

SALTED CHOCOLATE CHUNK COOKIES

Just a swift sprinkle of really good flaky sea salt, such as Maldon, adds a zing of flavor and unexpected crunch to rich, sweet chocolate-chunk cookies. This recipe makes enough to satisfy an entire classroom, and leftovers can be frozen for later.

1 Preheat the oven to 350°F. Line 2 baking sheets with parchment paper.

2 In a bowl, whisk together the flour, baking soda, and salt. Set aside.

3 In another bowl, combine the butter and both sugars. Beat with an electric mixer on low speed or by hand until combined, then beat on medium speed or briskly by hand until light and fluffy, about 3 minutes.

4 Add the eggs, one at a time, beating well after each addition. Add the vanilla and beat to combine. Gradually beat in the flour mixture on low speed or by hand, beating just until combined. Stir in the chocolate chunks until evenly combined.

5 Spoon nine 1½- to 2-inch balls of dough onto each prepared baking sheet, placing them at least 2 inches apart. Sprinkle the cookies evenly with the sea salt. Bake until lightly browned, 12–15 minutes. Let the cookies cool on the baking sheets for 5 minutes, then transfer to wire racks to cool completely. Repeat with the remaining dough.

prep time: 15 minutes
cooking time: 15 minutes

3¾ cups all-purpose flour

1¼ tsp baking soda

1 tsp salt

1¼ cups (2½ sticks) unsalted butter, at room temperature

1 cup firmly packed golden brown sugar

¾ cup granulated sugar

3 large eggs

2 tsp pure vanilla extract

1 bag (10–11½ oz) large chocolate chunks

Flaky sea salt for sprinkling

COWBOY COOKIES

Packed with oats, chocolate, coconut, and walnuts and baking up to more than four inches across, these bad boys meet all the requirements of the big cookie club. If you have time, refrigerate the dough for 30 minutes to 1 hour before or after shaping to prevent the cookies from spreading too much in the hot oven.

1 Preheat the oven to 350°F. Line 2 baking sheets with parchment paper.

2 In a bowl, mix the flour, baking powder, baking soda, cinnamon, and salt. Set aside.

3 In another bowl, beat the butter and both sugars with an electric mixer on medium speed or briskly by hand until light and fluffy, about 3 minutes. Reduce the speed to low and add the eggs, one at a time, beating well after each addition. Add the vanilla and beat until combined, about 1 minute. Add the flour mixture and beat on low speed or by hand until combined, about 1 minute. Stir in the oats, chocolate chips, coconut, and walnuts.

4 Drop the dough by rounded tablespoons onto the prepared baking sheets, spacing the cookies about 3 inches apart. Bake until the cookies are golden brown, 15–17 minutes. Transfer the cookies to a wire rack and let cool completely. Store the cookies in an airtight container at room temperature for up to 5 days.

prep time: 15 minutes
cooking time: 15 minutes

1½ cups all-purpose flour

2 tsp baking powder

1 tsp baking soda

1 tsp ground cinnamon

½ tsp kosher salt

¾ cup (1½ sticks) unsalted butter, at room temperature

¾ cup granulated sugar

¾ cup firmly packed dark brown sugar

2 large eggs

2 tsp pure vanilla extract

2 cups old-fashioned rolled oats

1 cup semisweet chocolate chips

¾ cup shredded dried unsweetened coconut

½ cup chopped walnuts

PEANUT BUTTER COOKIES

Finely chopped raw peanuts give these cookies extra peanutty flavor and texture. If chocolate is a prerequisite when it comes to sweets, dip the baked cookies into melted chocolate or add chocolate chips to the dough before baking. For a sugary crust, roll the dough balls in granulated sugar before pressing and baking.

1 Preheat the oven to 350°F. Line 2 baking sheets with parchment paper.

2 In a large bowl, beat the butter, both sugars, and peanut butter with an electric mixer on medium speed or briskly by hand until blended. Add the egg and vanilla and beat until blended. Add the flour, peanuts, baking soda, and salt and beat on low speed or by hand until blended.

3 Shape the dough into 1½-inch balls and place them at least 2 inches apart on the prepared baking sheets. Dip a fork in flour, then press twice into each cookie to make a crisscross pattern. Bake the cookies until golden,

8–10 minutes. Let the cookies cool on the baking sheets for 5 minutes, then transfer to wire racks and let cool completely.

4 If a chocolate dip is desired, combine the chocolate chips and shortening in a microwave-safe bowl. Microwave on high for 1 minute, stir gently, then microwave for 30 seconds longer, or until melted. One at a time, dip half of each cookie into the melted chocolate, then place on a baking sheet lined with parchment paper. When all the cookies are dipped, place the baking sheet in the refrigerator just until the chocolate is set, about 5 minutes. Store the cookies in an airtight container at room temperature for up to 5 days.

prep time: 15 minutes
cooking time: 10 minutes

½ cup (1 stick) unsalted butter, at room temperature

¾ cup firmly packed golden brown sugar

¼ cup granulated sugar

¾ cup creamy peanut butter

1 large egg

½ tsp pure vanilla extract

1¼ cups all-purpose flour

⅓ cup finely chopped unsalted raw peanuts

1 tsp baking soda

¼ tsp salt

FOR THE CHOCOLATE DIP (OPTIONAL)

1½ cups semisweet chocolate chips

1½ Tbsp vegetable shortening

NO-BAKE CHEESECAKE JARS

These single-serving cheesecakes are easy and delicious. Use a spoon to dig down to the graham cracker base, blending a bit of the crumbly crust, creamy middle, and fruity top in each bite. Screw on the jar tops to make them portable.

1 In a small bowl, combine the graham cracker crumbs, butter, and 2 Tbsp sugar until blended. Divide the mixture among 5 half-pint jars or 12-oz glasses, then use the blunt bottom end of a kitchen knife to tamp down the crumbs. Refrigerate until firm, 10–15 minutes.

2 Meanwhile, in a large bowl, beat the cream cheese and remaining ⅓ cup sugar with an electric mixer on medium speed or by hand until smooth. Beat in ¼ cup of the cream, the lemon juice, and the vanilla.

3 Put the water in a microwave-safe bowl. Sprinkle the gelatin over the surface and let soften for 2 minutes. Microwave on high until the gelatin dissolves, about 5 seconds. Remove from the microwave and stir in the remaining ¼ cup cream. Add the gelatin mixture to the cream cheese mixture and beat until fluffy, about 1 minute with an electric mixer on medium speed or 3 minutes by hand. Spoon the filling into the jars, dividing it evenly. Cover and refrigerate until firm, at least 1 hour or up to 2 days. Divide the fruit evenly among the jars before serving.

prep time: 10–15 minutes, plus at least 1 hour to chill

¾ cup graham cracker crumbs (from about 6 graham crackers)

2 Tbsp unsalted butter, at room temperature

2 Tbsp sugar plus ⅓ cup

1 lb cream cheese, at room temperature

½ cup heavy cream

1 Tbsp fresh lemon juice

½ tsp pure vanilla extract

1 Tbsp water

½ tsp unflavored gelatin

1 cup fresh sliced strawberries, raspberries, blueberries, blackberries, halved pitted cherries, or diced fresh peaches

PEACH-BLUEBERRY CRISP

Sliced peaches bake up soft and juicy underneath a crunchy oatmeal topping in this tasty crisp. Nectarines are a good sub for the peaches, as are blackberries for the blueberries. Vanilla ice cream provides a creamy counterpoint to the sweetness.

1 Preheat the oven to 375°F. In a small bowl, stir together the oats, sugar, flour, nuts, cinnamon, nutmeg, and salt. Using your fingertips, rub the butter into the oat mixture until well blended and crumbly.

2 In an 8-inch square baking dish or 9-inch round cake pan, combine the peaches and blueberries and spread in an even layer. Scatter the oat topping evenly over the fruit.

3 Bake until the juices are bubbling and the topping is richly browned, 30–35 minutes. Remove from the oven and let cool slightly. Serve warm or at room temperature, accompanied by vanilla ice cream, if desired.

prep time: 10 minutes
cooking time: 30 minutes

½ cup old-fashioned rolled oats

½ cup firmly packed golden brown sugar

¼ cup all-purpose flour

¼ cup finely chopped almonds or pecans

½ tsp ground cinnamon

¼ tsp ground nutmeg

¼ tsp salt

6 Tbsp unsalted butter, at room temperature

4 peaches, peeled, pitted, and sliced

1 cup blueberries

Vanilla ice cream for serving (optional)

PREPARATION TIP

To peel the peaches, blanch them in boiling water for 30 seconds, then use a slotted spoon to immediately transfer them to cold water. The peel should slip right off.

GLUTEN-FREE ALMOND CAKE

Unless you're looking for a workout with a whisk, this recipe is best made with an electric mixer since both the whites and the yolks need to be beaten until lofty. Line the pan bottom with parchment paper, or use a springform pan if you have one.

1 Preheat the oven to 350°F. Grease a 9-inch cake pan with butter, line the bottom with parchment paper, and grease the paper.

2 Separate the eggs, allowing the whites to drip into one bowl and placing the yolks in another bowl. Add the ¾ cup granulated sugar to the yolks and beat with an electric mixer or a whisk until pale yellow and creamy. Beat in the lemon zest and almond extract, then stir in the almond meal. Set aside.

3 Scoop 1 tsp of the egg whites and 1 tsp of the granulated sugar into a small bowl and beat with a fork until frothy. Add the almonds, toss to coat with the egg white mixture, and set aside.

4 Using a clean whisk or beaters, beat the remaining egg whites until frothy, then beat in the remaining 1 tsp granulated sugar and continue beating until stiff peaks form. Using a rubber spatula, stir one-quarter of the whipped egg whites into the yolk mixture to lighten it, then gently fold in the remaining egg whites in two batches. Pour the cake batter into the prepared pan.

5 Bake for 20 minutes. Sprinkle the reserved almonds evenly over the top and continue to bake until the cake is deep golden brown and pulls away from the pan sides, 10–12 minutes longer. Let cool in the pan for 10 minutes, then remove the cake from the pan, transfer to a wire rack and let cool completely. Just before serving, dust with powdered sugar.

prep time: 10 minutes
cooking time: 35 minutes

Butter for greasing

4 large eggs

¾ cup granulated sugar plus 2 teaspoons

¼ tsp grated lemon zest

½ tsp almond or vanilla extract

1 cup almond meal

½ cup sliced almonds

Powdered sugar for dusting

BLACKBERRY HAND PIES

Tastier than a pop tart, simpler than a whole pie, a pocket-size hand pie filled with sweet berries is hard to resist. For a glistening, crispy crust, brush the pastry with egg white and sprinkle with sugar before baking.

1 Unroll the pie crusts onto a lightly floured work surface. Using a 5-inch round plate as a guide, cut out 3 circles of dough from each pie crust. Discard the dough scraps or reserve for another use.

2 Line a baking sheet with parchment paper. In a bowl, toss together the blackberries, sugar, cornstarch, and salt. Transfer the dough rounds to the prepared baking sheet. Spoon one-sixth of the blackberry mixture over one side of a dough round, leaving a small border of dough uncovered around the edge. Using a small pastry brush, brush the border with the egg white. Fold the uncovered dough over the blackberries,

pressing gently along the border to seal the blackberries inside. Using the tines of a fork, press along the rim to seal the edge. Repeat to fill and seal the remaining rounds.

3 Refrigerate the mini pies on the baking sheet until the dough is firm, 15–20 minutes. Meanwhile, preheat the oven to 375°F.

4 Brush each pie with the egg white and sprinkle lightly with sugar. Bake until golden, 35–40 minutes. Let the pies cool slightly on the baking sheet on a wire rack. Serve warm or at room temperature. Store any leftover pies in a covered container at room temperature for up to 2 days.

prep time: 25 minutes
cooking time: 40 minutes

---

2 store-bought rolled refrigerated pie crusts for a 9-inch pie

All-purpose flour for dusting

1 pint (about 1½ cups) blackberries

3 Tbsp sugar, plus more for sprinkling

2 Tbsp cornstarch

Pinch salt

1 large egg white, lightly beaten, for brushing

CLASSIC TARTE TATIN

Use any good baking apple, such as Golden Delicious, Pink Lady, or Granny Smith, for this caramelized upside-down apple pie. You'll need an oven-safe frying pan for first cooking the apples and then baking them with the pie crust.

1 Preheat the oven to 375°F. In a large oven-safe frying pan, melt the butter over medium heat. Sprinkle the sugar evenly over the melted butter and continue cooking until the sugar melts and turns amber colored, 3–4 minutes. Swirl the pan frequently to redistribute the sugar. Arrange the apples in the bottom of the pan, placing them in overlapping concentric circles that form a snug, even layer. Increase the heat to medium-high and cook until the apples are just tender, about 15 minutes. The caramel will bubble up around the apples. Remove the pan from the heat.

2 When the bubbling has subsided, unroll the pastry round and place it on top of the apples, tucking in the edges and being careful not to burn your fingers. Bake until the crust is golden brown, about 30 minutes. Let cool on a wire rack for 5 minutes.

3 Place a large flat plate upside down on the pan and invert the pan and plate together. Lift off the pan. Serve the tart warm with vanilla ice cream, if you like.

prep time: 10 minutes
cooking time: 50 minutes

¼ cup (½ stick) unsalted butter, cut into pieces

¾ cup sugar

5 apples, about 2 lb, peeled, cored, and thickly sliced

1 store-bought rolled refrigerated pie crust for a 9-inch pie

Vanilla ice cream for serving (optional)

PUFF PASTRY FRUIT TARTS

A sheet of frozen puff pastry, some fresh fruit, and a sprinkling of sugar is all that's needed to create flaky, buttery, professional-looking fruit tarts in just minutes. For variety, add a sprinkling of chopped nuts or fresh herb leaves just before serving.

1 Preheat the oven to 400°F. Line a baking sheet with parchment paper.

2 On a lightly floured work surface, unfold the pastry sheet and press flat, pinching closed any broken seams. Cut the pastry sheet into 4 equal squares and place well apart on the prepared baking sheet. Top each square with an equal amount of the sliced fruit, arranging the slices attractively and leaving a ½-inch border around the edges uncovered. Sprinkle each square evenly with 1 tablespoon sugar.

3 Bake until the fruit is tender and the pastry is golden brown, 15–20 minutes. Serve warm or at room temperature.

prep time: 5 minutes
cooking time: 15 minutes

***

All-purpose flour for dusting

1 sheet frozen puff pastry, thawed but still very cold

¾ lb pitted apricots, plums, or peaches, or cored and peeled apples, cut into ½-inch wedges

4 Tbsp sugar

HONEY-ROASTED PEACH WITH ICE CREAM & GRANOLA

Caramelized and crisp on the outside, juicy and hot on the inside, roasted peaches are the bomb. Ice cream offers extra moisture and sweetness, while a sprinkling of granola provides a little crunch. If you're serving friends, add to the number of peaches and figure the additional ingredients accordingly.

1 Preheat the oven to 400°F. Line a small baking dish with aluminum foil and brush the foil with melted butter.

2 In a small cup, mix the sugar and vanilla. Place the peach halves, skin side down, in the prepared pan. Drizzle evenly with the honey, sprinkle with the sugar mixture, and top with the butter, dividing it equally.

3 Roast until tender and browned, about 20 minutes.

4 Transfer to a small serving bowl. Pour any fruit juices from the pan over the peach, then drizzle on the remaining honey. Top with a scoop of ice cream, sprinkle with the granola, and serve.

prep time: 10 minutes
cooking time: 20 minutes

2 tsp unsalted butter, plus melted butter for baking dish

1 Tbsp firmly packed golden brown sugar

¼ tsp pure vanilla extract

1 large peach, halved and pitted

1 Tbsp honey

Vanilla ice cream or whipped cream for serving

1 Tbsp Awesome Granola (page 16) or store-bought granola

COCONUT-CHOCOLATE-ALMOND RICE CRISPY TREATS

These chocolate-studded almond and coconut squares are something like a tasty blend of a favorite childhood candy bar and a beloved bake sale treat. Melt the marshmallows on the stovetop or take a shortcut and melt them in the microwave.

1 Butter a 13 x 9-inch baking dish or rimmed baking sheet.

2 Melt the butter in a large saucepan over low heat. Add the marshmallows and stir until completely melted, about 3 minutes. Remove from the heat. Add the cereal, coconut, and almonds and stir just until evenly mixed. Add the chocolate chips and stir to distribute evenly.

3 Using wet hands or a greased spatula, evenly press the mixture into the prepared baking dish. Let stand until set, then cut into generous squares.

prep time: 10 minutes

3 Tbsp butter, plus more for greasing

1 package (10 oz) regular marshmallows or 4 cups mini marshmallows

6 cups crisped rice cereal

1 cup sweetened shredded coconut

½ cup sliced or chopped almonds, toasted

1½ cups semisweet chocolate chips

MICROWAVE IT

In a microwave-safe bowl, combine the butter and marshmallows. Microwave on high for 2 minutes, stir well, then continue to microwave until the marshmallows are melted, 1 minute longer. Stir until smooth. Continue as directed to mix in the remaining ingredients.

INDIVIDUAL NUTELLA SOUFFLÉS

Mix Nutella with egg yolks, then lighten it with egg whites, for über-easy soufflés.

1 Preheat the oven to 375°F. Butter two ½-cup ramekins or small ovenproof cups, then dust with sugar, turning to coat them evenly.

2 In a bowl, whisk the egg whites until frothy. Sprinkle the 1 tsp sugar over the egg whites and continue whisking until firm, moist peaks form. In another bowl, using a spatula, stir the egg yolks into the Nutella, then stir in one-third of the whites. Gently fold in the remaining whites until blended. Divide the mixture between the ramekins.

3 Bake until risen and set on top but still moist in the centers, about 15 minutes. Serve at once.

prep time: 10 minutes
cooking time: 15 minutes

Butter for greasing

1 tsp sugar, plus more for dusting

2 large eggs, separated

½ cup Nutella

CHOCOLATE MUG CAKE

This single-serving cake-in-a-cup is the best quick fix for a chocolate craving.

1 In an 8-oz coffee cup, mix the flour, sugar, cocoa powder, and baking powder. Add the milk and canola oil. Stir until blended. Scatter the chocolate chips evenly over the top.

2 Microwave on high for 1 minute, then leave in the microwave with the door closed for 2 minutes before eating. The cake should be moist but cooked throughout.

prep time: 2 minutes
cooking time: 3 minutes

3 Tbsp all-purpose flour

2 Tbsp firmly packed brown sugar

1 Tbsp unsweetened cocoa powder

¼ tsp baking powder

3 Tbsp milk

1 Tbsp canola oil

1 Tbsp semisweet chocolate chips

DRESSED-UP BROWNIES FROM A BOX

Elegant with marbleized swirls of cream cheese, or campfire cool with toasted marshmallows and crisp graham crackers, or perky with crushed peppermint, these amped-up brownies from a box are sure to impress.

1 Preheat the oven to 350°F. Butter a 9 x 13-inch baking pan.

2 Make the brownie batter according to the package directions. Pour into the prepared pan and proceed as directed below for the selected preparation.

prep time: 5 minutes
cooking time: 30 minutes

━━━━━━━━━━

1 box (about 22 oz) store-bought brownie mix (for a 9 x 13-inch pan), plus any ingredients required

---

VARIATIONS

Black Bottom
In a small bowl, whisk 8 oz cream cheese, 1 large egg, ⅓ cup sugar, and ½ tsp pure vanilla extract until blended; set aside. Make the brownie batter as directed. Scrape the batter into the prepared pan and spread evenly. Spoon the cream cheese mixture over the top. Using a chopstick or knife, gently swirl the chocolate and cream cheese batters together in a series of figure eights. Bake as directed.

S'More
Make the brownie batter and bake as directed. About 10–12 minutes before the end of baking, crush 6 graham crackers with your hands and scatter evenly over the top. Place 12 jumbo marshmallows over the graham crackers, spacing them evenly. Continue baking until the marshmallows are golden brown, 10–14 minutes.

Peppermint Crunch
Make the brownie batter as directed but mix in 2 tsp peppermint extract. Bake as directed. Meanwhile, put 1 cup unwrapped hard peppermint candies in a large heavy-duty lock-top plastic bag. Seal the bag closed and, using a meat pounder or hammer, crush the candies into small pieces. About 10–12 minutes before the end of baking, sprinkle the crushed candies evenly over the brownie batter. Continue baking as directed.

THE BASICS

SIDES

Steamed White Rice

MAKES 3 CUPS

1 cup long-grain white rice, such as jasmine
or basmati
1½ cups water
¼ tsp salt

In a saucepan, bring the rice, water, and salt to a boil over high heat. Reduce the heat to low, give the rice a stir, then cover and cook, without lifting the lid, until the liquid is absorbed and the rice is tender, 20 minutes. Remove from the heat and let stand, covered, for 10 minutes. Uncover, fluff with a fork, and serve.

cooking time: 20 minutes

Steamed Brown Rice

MAKES 3 CUPS

1 cup short-grain brown rice
2 cups water
¼ tsp salt

In a saucepan, bring the rice, water, and salt to a boil over high heat. Reduce the heat to low, give the rice a stir, then cover and cook, without lifting the lid, until the liquid is absorbed and the rice is tender, 45–50 minutes. Remove from the heat and let stand, covered, for 10 minutes. Uncover, fluff with a fork, and serve.

cooking time: 45 minutes

Cooked Farro

MAKES 3 CUPS

1 cup farro, either whole (with husk and bran),
semi-pearled (no husk and polished to remove some bran),
or pearled (all bran removed)

Put the farro in a small saucepan and cover with water by about 2 inches. Bring to a boil over high heat, then reduce the heat to medium-low, cover, and simmer until tender, about 20 minutes for pearled, 30 minutes for semipearled, and 40 minutes for whole. Drain off any excess water, fluff with a fork, and serve.

cooking time: 20 minutes

Cooked Quinoa

MAKES 3 CUPS

1 cup quinoa, rinsed well
2 cups water or low-sodium chicken broth
½ tsp salt

Stovetop: Put the quinoa in a saucepan and stir in the water and salt. Bring to a boil over high heat, then cover, reduce the heat to low, and steam until tender, about 15 minutes. Remove from the heat and let stand, covered, for 5 minutes longer.

cooking time: 15 minutes

Microwave: Put the quinoa in a microwave-safe bowl or dish, add the water, and stir to mix. Cover and microwave on high for 6 minutes. Stir to break up any clumps. Cover and continue to microwave on high until tender and the water is absorbed, about 2 minutes longer. Let stand in the microwave for 2 more minutes. Uncover and fluff with a fork. If the mixture seems wet, keep covered and let steam until all the moisture is incorporated.

cooking time: 10 minutes

Mashed Potatoes

MAKES 8–10 SERVINGS

3 lb russet, Yukon Gold, or sweet potatoes,
peeled and cut into chunks
Salt and ground white pepper
½ cup (1 stick) unsalted butter,
at room temperature
About ½ cup whole milk, warmed

Stovetop: Put the potatoes in a large saucepan and cover with salted water. Bring to a boil over high heat. Reduce the heat to medium-low and simmer until the potatoes are tender when pierced with a knife, about 20 minutes. Drain well. Return the potatoes to the pan and stir over medium-low heat for 2 minutes to evaporate the excess moisture. Mash the potatoes with a potato masher, fork, or electric mixer; do not overmix. Cut the butter into slices and scatter over the potatoes. Whisk in the butter and enough warm milk to produce the desired texture. Season to taste with salt and white pepper, and serve.

prep time: 15 minutes | cooking time: 22 minutes

Microwave: Put the potato chunks in a colander, rinse with cold running water, and transfer to a microwave-safe bowl. Cover with microwavable plastic wrap and poke a few vents in the top. Microwave on high until tender, 9–11 minutes. Remove the bowl from the microwave and let stand, covered, for a few minutes to steam. Meanwhile, in a small microwave-safe bowl or glass measuring cup, combine ¾ cup milk with ¼ cup (½ stick) unsalted butter and microwave on high until the milk is warm and the butter is melted, about 1 minute. Pour the milk mixture over the potatoes and mash to the desired texture, adding more milk or butter if needed.

prep time: 15 minutes | cooking time: 10 minutes

Winter Squash Purée

MAKES 2–3 CUPS

1 winter squash, such as acorn, butternut, or kabocha, seeded, halved lengthwise, and seeds removed
Olive oil for drizzling
Salt and pepper

Oven: Preheat the oven to 400°F. Drizzle the squash halves with olive oil, rub to coat the cut surfaces, and season to taste with salt and pepper. Place, cut side down, on a baking sheet. Bake until fork-tender, 35–45 minutes for acorn, 40–50 minutes for butternut, and 45–55 minutes for kabocha. Set aside until cool enough to handle, then scoop out the squash flesh with a spoon. Use as directed in individual recipes.

prep time: 5 minutes | cooking time: 35 minutes

Microwave: Microwave one squash half at a time. Drizzle a squash half with olive oil, rub to coat the cut surface, and season with salt and pepper. Place the squash half, cut side down, on a microwave-safe plate. Microwave on high power until fork-tender, about 6 minutes for acorn, 10 minutes for butternut, and 11 minutes for kabocha. If the squash is not yet tender at the end of the cooking time, continue to cook in 30-second intervals until done. Set aside until cool enough to handle, then scoop out the squash flesh with a spoon. Repeat with the other half. Use as directed in individual recipes.

prep time: 5 minutes | cooking time: 6 minutes

Cooked Bacon

MAKES 2–8 BACON STRIPS

2–8 bacon strips

Stovetop: In a frying pan over medium heat, cook the bacon, turning as needed, until crisp, about 8 minutes.

cooking time: 8 minutes

Microwave: Line a microwave-safe baking dish with 4 layers of paper towels. Lay the bacon strips in a single layer on top. (Use 4 strips for the best results.) Cover with 2 layers of paper towels and microwave on high until crisped, about 1 minute per slice. Remove the paper towels just after cooking or it will stick to the bacon.

cooking time: 1–8 minutes

Cooked Chicken

MAKES 1–2 COOKED CHICKEN BREASTS

1–2 boneless, skinless chicken breasts
¼–½ tsp salt
¼ tsp black peppercorns
1 smashed garlic clove
4 fresh herb sprigs, such as thyme or parsley

Put the chicken in a single layer in a saucepan. Add water to cover by 1–2 inches. Add the salt, peppercorns, garlic, and herbs. Bring to a boil over medium-high heat, then immediately reduce the heat to low, cover, and simmer until the chicken is opaque throughout, 10–14 minutes. Transfer the chicken to a cutting board and let cool, then use as directed.

cooking time: 10 minutes

VINAIGRETTES

Basic Vinaigrette

MAKES ABOUT ¼ CUP

1 Tbsp white wine vinegar or red wine vinegar
3–4 Tbsp extra-virgin olive oil
Salt and pepper to taste

In a jar with a lid, combine all the ingredients. Cover and shake until well blended. Use right away, or cover and refrigerate for up to 1 week.

prep time: 5 minutes

Thai Vinaigrette

MAKES ABOUT ⅓ CUP

1½ Tbsp rice vinegar
1 Tbsp fresh lime juice
1 Tbsp fish sauce
1½ tsp soy sauce
1½ tsp toasted sesame oil
½ tsp sugar
¼–½ tsp Sriracha, or to taste
1 clove garlic, minced

In a jar with a lid, combine all the ingredients.
Cover and shake until well blended. Use right
away, or cover and refrigerate for up to 1 week.

prep time: 5 minutes

SAUCES & DIPS

Guacamole

MAKES ABOUT 2½ CUPS

3 ripe avocados, halved and pitted
Juice of 1 lime
Salt and ground black pepper
1–2 dashes hot pepper sauce, such as Tabasco
(optional)
3 Tbsp chopped fresh cilantro (optional)

Using a spoon, scoop the flesh of the avocado into
a bowl. Add the lime juice and mash with a fork to the
desired consistency. Season with salt, pepper, and hot
pepper sauce (if using). Stir in the cilantro (if using) and
serve. To store, transfer to an airtight container. Dampen
a paper towel with water and press gently over the
surface of the guacamole, then cover and refrigerate
for up to 2 days.

prep time: 10 minutes

VARIATION
Chunky Guacamole: Pit, peel, and cut 3 avocados
into ½-inch cubes and put in a bowl. Add 2 Roma
tomatoes, cut into small dice; 3 Tbsp finely chopped
red onion; ¼ cup chopped fresh cilantro; the juice
of 1 lime; and 1 small jalapeño chile, seeded and
minced. Gently toss. Season with salt and pepper.

prep time: 15 minutes

Fresh Tomato Salsa

MAKES ¾ CUP

2 Roma tomatoes
¼ white onion, finely diced
2 Tbsp finely chopped fresh cilantro
½ tsp salt, or as needed

Cut the tomatoes in half crosswise and squeeze out the
seeds. Dice the tomatoes finely. Put in a bowl and add
the onion, cilantro, and salt. Stir to mix well, taste, and
adjust the seasoning. Serve right away, or cover and
refrigerate for up to 3 days.

prep time: 10 minutes

Pineapple Salsa

MAKES ABOUT 3½ CUPS

½ pineapple, peeled, cored, and diced (about 2½ cups)
⅓ cup loosely packed fresh cilantro leaves, chopped
¼ cup finely chopped red onion
1 small red jalapeño chile, seeded and minced
2 Tbsp olive oil
1 Tbsp lime juice
Salt and pepper

In a nonreactive bowl, mix the pineapple, cilantro,
onion, jalapeño, olive oil, and lime juice. Season with
salt and pepper. Let stand at room temperature for
about 15 minutes, stirring once or twice. Serve right
away, or cover and refrigerate for up to 1 day.

prep time: 20 minutes

Salsa Verde

MAKES ⅔ CUP

2 large cloves garlic, pressed
¼ tsp salt
3 Tbsp olive oil
1 Tbsp fresh lime juice
¼ bunch fresh flat-leaf parsley, minced
¼ bunch fresh cilantro, minced
½ tsp ground black pepper
¼ tsp red pepper flakes

In a small bowl, mash the garlic with the salt, using
the back of a spoon, until a paste forms. Stir in the oil,
lime juice, parsley, cilantro, black pepper, and red

pepper flakes. Store leftovers in an airtight container and cover with a thin layer of olive oil to slow discoloration. Refrigerate for up to 1 week.

prep time: 10 minutes

Hummus

MAKES ABOUT 3 CUPS

2 cans (15 oz each) chickpeas, drained and rinsed
½ cup lemon juice, or as needed
½ cup tahini
4 Tbsp extra-virgin olive oil
5 cloves garlic, minced
¼ tsp ground cumin
¾ tsp salt, or as needed

In a food processor or blender, combine the chickpeas, lemon juice, tahini, 3 Tbsp of the oil, the garlic, cumin, and salt. Process until a soft, creamy paste forms. Taste and adjust the seasoning with salt and lemon juice, if needed. Transfer to a serving bowl and drizzle with the remaining 1 Tbsp oil. Serve right away, or cover and refrigerate for up to 4 days.

prep time: 10 minutes

White Pizza Sauce

MAKES 1¼ CUPS

2 Tbsp olive oil
½ yellow onion, minced
3 cloves garlic, minced
Salt and pepper
1 cup whole-milk ricotta cheese
¼ cup heavy cream
1 tsp fresh oregano leaves or ½ tsp dried oregano

In a small frying pan, warm the oil over medium heat. Add the onion, garlic, and a pinch each of salt and pepper. Cook, stirring, until the onion is translucent, 3–4 minutes. Transfer the contents of the pan to a bowl and let cool. When the onion mixture is cool, stir in the ricotta, cream, and oregano. Taste and season with more salt and pepper, if needed. Use right away, or store in an airtight container in the refrigerator for up to 1 week or in the freezer for up to 2 months.

prep time: 5 minutes | cooking time: 5 minutes

Microwave Cranberry Sauce

MAKES ABOUT 2 CUPS

12 oz cranberries, fresh or frozen
1 cup sugar
½ cup orange juice or water

Put the cranberries in a microwave-safe bowl or dish. Sprinkle over the sugar, then add the orange juice. Cover with microwavable plastic wrap vented on the sides. Microwave on high until the berries pop, about 7 minutes. Let stand, covered, until cool. Serve right away, or cover and refrigerate for up to 1 week.

cooking time: 7 minutes

Blue Cheese Dip & Dressing

MAKES ABOUT 1½ CUPS

1 cup crumbled blue cheese
¾ cup sour cream
½ cup mayonnaise
1 large clove garlic, minced
2 tsp Worcestershire sauce
Whole milk, as needed

In a bowl, blend the blue cheese, sour cream, mayonnaise, garlic, and Worcestershire sauce. Thin with milk to the desired texture. Serve right away, or cover and refrigerate for up to 4 days.

prep time: 5 minutes

Chile Dipping Sauce

MAKES ABOUT ¼ CUP

¼ cup fresh lime juice
2 Tbsp firmly packed brown sugar
2 Tbsp fish sauce
1 Tbsp rice vinegar
1 Tbsp chopped cilantro
⅛ tsp dried red pepper flakes

In a small bowl, whisk together all the ingredients. Let stand for 5 minutes before serving.

prep time: 3 minutes

Index

THE COLLEGE COOKBOOK
Produced by Weldon Owen.

WELDON OWEN
President & Publisher Roger Shaw
SVP, Sales & Marketing Amy Kaneko
Finance & Operations Director Thomas Morgan

Associate Publisher Amy Marr
Senior Editor & Recipe Developer Lisa Atwood

Creative Director Kelly Booth
Art Director Marisa Kwek
Production Designer Howie Severson

Production Director Michelle Duggan
Production Manager Sam Bissell
Imaging Manager Don Hill

Photographer Aubrie Pick
Food Stylist Fanny Pan
Prop Stylist Claire Mack

ACKNOWLEDGMENTS
Weldon Owen wishes to thank the following
people for their generous support in producing this
book: Rizwan A. Alvi, Lauren Arendt, Summer
Atwood, Lisa Berman, Lesley Bruynesteyn, Lou
Bustamante, Allister Fein, Bessma Khalaf, Kristene
Loayza, Rachel Markowitz, Florie Maschmeyer,
Alexis Mersel, Scottie Milagro, Lucie Parker,
Elizabeth Parson, Molly O'Neil Stewart,
and Karen Wise.

Chapter openers Instagram photo credits Rizwan
A. Alvi (page: 11, 37, 53, 72, 73 & 102), Summer
Atwood (page: 36, 37, 53, 72 & 103),
Lisa Berman (page: 37), Kelly Booth (page: 11, 37, 52,
53 & 103), Lou Bustamante (page: 52), Allister Fein
(page: 11, 53, 72, 73 & 102), Amy Marr (page: 36
& 52), Scottie Milagro (page: 11, 36, 37, 52 & 53), Alexis
Mersel (page: 11), Molly O'Neil Stewart
(page: 103), Lucie Parker (page: 10 & 53),
and Aubrie Pick (page: 10 & 73).

A WELDON OWEN PRODUCTION
P.O. Box 3088
San Rafael, CA 94912
www.weldonowen.com

Copyright © 2018 Weldon Owen

All rights reserved, including
the right of reproduction in whole or
in part in any form.

Printed and bound in China.

First printed in 2018
10 9 8 7 6 5 4 3

Library of Congress Cataloging-
in-Publication data is available.

ISBN-13: 978-1-68188-436-3